KU-218-723

From The Women's Press Ltd
34 Great Sutton Street, London EC1V 0DX

Mary Evans is senior lecturer in sociology at the University of Kent, where she helped to set up the first women's studies postgraduate degree in Britain. She is the author of *The Woman Question* (Fontana, 1982), and of three books published by Tavistock Publications Ltd, *Simone de Beauvoir: A Feminist Mandarin* (1985), *Jane Austen and the State* (1987) and *Reflecting on Anna Karenina* (1989). She lives in Canterbury.

MARY EVANS

A Good School

Life at a Girls' Grammar School in the 1950s

With a preface by Baroness Blackstone

The Women's Press

First published by The Women's Press Limited 1991
A member of the Namara Group
34 Great Sutton Street, London EC1V 0DX

British Library in Cataloguing in Publication Data

Evans, Mary
   A good school: life at a girls' grammar school in the
   1950s.
   1. Great Britain. Girls' schools, history
   I. Title
   376.941

   ISBN 0-7043-4268-5

Typeset by MC Typeset Ltd, Gillingham, Kent

Printed and bound in Great Britain by Cox & Wyman,
Reading, Berks

To Pat Macpherson,
a wonderful teacher

Contents

Acknowledgments

I am very grateful to those people who helped me with the writing of this book, as teachers and friends. I owe special debts to a teacher of history, Miss J. Howard, whose interest in her subject was endlessly engaging and to Ralph Miliband, whose patience with a product of a grammar school education was illuminating. Pat Macpherson was kind enough to read and comment on the manuscript and Sue Macdonald typed it with her customary skill and speed.

Preface

Mary Evans' book *A Good School: Life at a Girls' Grammar School in the 1950s* is a fascinating, and a timely, book to read. Amongst other things it provides an important insight into the failings of the selective system of education at a time when selection may re-emerge as a consequence of the Education Reform Act.

Mary Evans went to a girls' grammar school between 1956 and 1963. She does not disclose where it was, she names no one and avoids vignettes of individual pupils or teachers. Instead she describes the institution in general terms as an ideal/typical model of the genre during the 1950s and early 1960s. She writes in the first person plural from the perspective of 'we, the pupils', although occasionally she refers to the views of parents and indeed of the teachers themselves. Her account is cool and analytical and never at any point tinged with sentiment or nostalgia. She applies the tools of the social scientist in dissecting the goals of the institution and examining how they were pursued. At the same time it is not a dispassionate account. The perspective is of a critic, discerning, yet none the less hostile towards much that the girls' grammar school of the period stood for and dismissive about the methods it employed. It is a standpoint that not everyone will share, but which helps to make this book an excellent read.

Thousands of middle-aged women shared Mary Evans' single-sex grammar school experience. Not all of them would interpret the experience in quite the same way, which is why the book is challenging. I am one of those thousands. I went to a girls' grammar school too and I loved it – at least for most of the time.

I arrived at Ware Grammar School for Girls a little before my eleventh birthday in September 1953 and stayed there until July 1960. I had come from a Roman Catholic private school, attached to a convent of the Sisters of Mercy, and many of the teachers were nuns. It taught me to read, write and spell with great efficiency, and I learned my tables like a parrot, but it failed to provide me with any understanding of the simplest of mathematical concepts. For me the highlight of the week was the ballet classes, a paid-for extra provided by a visiting teacher, where I acquired my passion for ballet – for that I am enormously grateful. Otherwise I did not enjoy it much: discipline was severe; conformity required; eccentricity of any kind ridiculed. Its values were petit bourgeois in the extreme. After this the grammar school seemed liberating.

The first benefit it provided was subject specialists: teachers with degrees in the subjects they taught. This meant variety each day of the week: there were young teachers, as well as middle-aged teachers, married and unmarried teachers, good, bad and indifferent teachers. Some were imaginative and flexible in the teaching methods they used; others were rigid or dull or both.

The teaching of English was one of the school's strengths and I suspect that may have been fairly typical. My experience in this respect was quite different from that of Mary Evans. While old fashioned grammar lessons may not have been of much value, I doubt whether they actually prevented pupils from writing well. The girls' grammar school of the period undoubtedly failed in a number of respects, but teaching their pupils to write was something they did relatively well. Similarly, the teaching of English literature had, in my experience, much less of the Gradgrind character than is described in this book. Many girls read widely, as well as acquiring some understanding of literary criticism. In my own school, as a measure – probably unusual – to increase the range and number of novels, plays and poems we read, English literature was not taken as an O level subject because of its narrow range. That English was a popular subject was reflected in the numbers who took it at A level.

The failures, I believe, were in other areas. The physical

sciences were often poorly taught and there were even then shortages of teachers of these subjects in girls' schools. Although I wanted to take science subjects at O level I was discouraged from doing so and channelled into languages and other arts subjects, having to make do with biology only. I am woefully ignorant of even the most basic principles of the physical sciences. Many girls also failed to pass O level Mathematics, although I struggled through. Since grammar schools were teaching only the top 25 per cent of the ability range in most parts of Britain it was a shameful failure to turn so many bright girls out into the world without even sufficient mathematical skills and understanding to pass the subject at O level. Those who criticise comprehensive schools sometimes conveniently forget these failures, let alone how dismal the educational experiences of most secondary modern pupils were.

The low status attached to any practical or vocational skills was another problem. Mary Evans is especially good when talking about the teaching of domestic science and needlework. She describes in some detail the pointlessness of spending a year smocking a pinafore – what she calls 'education in the thankless task'. My own experience was not dissimilar: needlework was compulsory only in the second year; but the entire year was dedicated to making a green cotton needlework bag, identical for each pupil. To distinguish one's bag from those of other pupils, it was therefore considered necessary to embroider one's name on this ghastly object in orange silk. The Jill Smiths and Ann Webbs were in luck; those of us with longer names suffered more. The second syllable of my surname was never completed. The asinine nature of this task became even more apparent when most girls gave up the subject at the end of the year and the then useless object we had laboured over for so long was consigned to the dustbin. How much more useful it would have been if we had learned how to mend a fuse, put on a plug or lengthen a piece of electric wire; or even far more valuable had we spent the time learning to type.

Many grammar schools of the period went in for rigid streaming, based on performance in the eleven plus examination; or in some cases after assessing children at the end of their first year at secondary school. Here my own school was more enlightened; there was no streaming, although there were sets for English, French and Mathematics from the third to the fifth year. In these circumstances the culture of failure which could so easily develop in the bottom streams and which was brilliantly analysed in David Hargreaves' book *Social Relations in a Secondary School* (Routledge & Kegan Paul, 1967), could not flourish in quite the way described by Mary Evans. It was certainly a mistaken doctrine that mixed ability teaching was inferior to streaming in schools that had already selected in terms of ability at entry. And I entirely endorse what the author of this book says about the undesirable effects of streaming on those in the lower streams. It should be noted, however, that not all grammar schools did use streaming.

They did, though, with very few exceptions, insist on a school uniform. I have never forgotten the incredulity of some European visitors, unfamiliar with the British school system, at the sight of hundreds of identically dressed adolescent girls pouring out of school. As a parent I am not in favour of uniforms; having had one child in a school with them and one without I can vouch for the much greater peace of mind the latter state provided. There are plenty of other things to fight about with adolescents, and disputes about ties, blazers and berets seem to me a pointless addition to the list. Yet I cannot agree with Mary Evans that the cost of most grammar school uniforms was as high as she implies; nor in most places were the outfitters located far from the school. I do accept that for the very poor, blazers and ties represented a burdensome additional cost, without which they would have been better off. As the author says, uniforms were the distinguishing feature of the selective secondary school, making their pupils identifiable in the world beyond the school gates, and separating them from their less successful peers in the secondary modern schools.

Adolescent girls discovering their sexuality can easily become obsessed with their appearance. Was the girls' grammar school 30 years ago wrong to play this down? I am not sure: focusing attention on virtues other than that of dressing well is surely no bad thing. Certainly questions about sex and what constitutes sexual attraction should have been addressed more directly, as Mary Evans argues. An interest in sex should not have been interpreted as a sign of being unserious about study. That it often was, created guilty fears and conflicts in many teenagers struggling to please teachers, parents and peers. I was surprised by Mary Evans' portrayal of the fears surrounding lesbians and lesbianism; I myself do not remember it ever being discussed, nor that I or most of my peers were more than vaguely aware of its existence.

The view of the world gained from these schools was perhaps a little too cosy, and there was not much opportunity to challenge the values they represented. The quality of the teaching was very variable, and in general rather unimaginative. However, for many pupils the overall experience was quite enjoyable. As well as formal lessons there were plays to be performed, choirs in which to sing and various sports to be pursued. Friends were made. And although there was some drudgery, in my experience there was also plenty of fun. In my opinion the greatest failure of these schools, in contrast to grammar schools for boys, was that their expectations for their pupils' post-school destinations were too low. Teaching, nursing and secretarial work were the norms, and little effort went into encouraging even the brightest pupils to raise their aspirations or consider less conventional alternatives. As a result plenty of female talent was wasted. What a pity.

Tessa Blackstone
August 1990

1

The Culture of the School

In *Brideshead Revisited* Evelyn Waugh remarks, through his narrator, Charles Ryder, that 'his theme is memory'. This preoccupation is justified because, Ryder remarks, 'memory is all that we have'. When Charles Ryder is left with nothing except memories of the Brideshead family that he had known and loved he finds the world in which he lives impoverished and alien. Indeed, throughout the novel Ryder has seen all other characters through the filter of the values and habits of the Brideshead family: his wife is not Julia, his friends and business associates have none of the taste or the familiarity with the heights of western culture that he took for granted amongst the Brideshead clan. The departed, disunited world of Brideshead acts as a point of comparison for all that Ryder encounters in his adult life. His banishment from this world leads him further into what is at best an uncomfortable accommodation to his circumstances.

Memory in this particular account has then the force to colour perception and judgment. Charles Ryder may have fallen for a family that other readers may not have found attractive – a pompous brother, a drunken brother, a sanctimonious sister and mother are not to everyone's taste – but what Charles Ryder finds endlessly seductive is less important than the effect that the attraction has on his life. So with all memories of a golden past: the elements that constitute the past are frequently misrepresented and misconstructed; the force of memory is its power to colour and structure our present actions and interpretations of the real world. Memories, both individual and collective, thus form part of the social thought of any age and their force to mobilise and influence are evident in the history of every western society. Yet as Raphael Samuel and others have recently pointed out in their critiques of the 'heritage' and 'golden days of industrialisation' industries, the interpretation of the past becomes all too easily a distortion of the actual social and personal relationships that dominated the lives of the majority of the population.

But few of us have the opportunity to offer a socially agreed and accepted version of the past, and many of us have to live within the definitions of the past of its interpreters. Throughout all classes and groups in British society there exists a nostalgia for the past. People are nostalgic about different things, but certain common themes about the past are, perhaps, detectable in a fairly general sense in contemporary British society. Among these themes is the belief in the greater degree of social order and cohesion in the past. It was a world in which children respected their parents (preferably the authority of their fathers) and their teachers, a place in which the urban world was safe – particularly for women – and a place in which certain standards and attitudes could be taken for granted. It is impossible to know whether or not these attitudes have actually changed; what is socially and ideologically significant is anyway less the actual change than the perception of the change. It is with one aspect of the perception of the changed world that this book is concerned – the belief that English grammar schools were educational institutions of great value in which well-behaved children learned useful things and went on to make the kind of orderly and productive contribution to society that is so often absent today. Grammar schools are, I shall argue, the Brideshead of Conservative – and conservative – educational thinking. They represent the golden age of state education, their demise is seen as the point at which English state schools started to go irretrievably downhill and towards those urban comprehensives which offer unfamiliar subjects and a curriculum, both formal and informal, which is at odds with all 'proper' expectations of social order. In short, the perception of many recent Secretaries of State for Education suggests a transformation of the agenda of schools from order to disorder, from the form of structured learning which so delights examiners to the haphazard accumulation of facts through projects and exercises which may sharpen the wits but does not teach an orderly attitude to knowledge.

But memories of education, like Charles Ryder's memory of the past, are not necessarily reliable. Of course there were excellent grammar schools, and no doubt they produced happy, well-educated pupils. At the same time these excellent schools produced unhappy, badly educated pupils, for whom education-as-they-knew-it was never more or less than daily, forced interaction of the unwilling and resentful. The point, therefore, is not that grammar schools were 'good' or 'bad' in any final sense, but that our evaluation of education, and its results, is so subjective in certain crucial respects as to be entirely unreliable. When grammar schools are praised as the schools which produced well-organised and literate pupils, the argument obscures the educational successes that the grammar schools *failed* to produce: not just the vast majority of that generation which anyway attended secondary modern schools rather than grammar schools, but the other 90 per cent of the intake of the grammar schools which did not go on to higher education or professional training. Comprehensive schools with large sixth forms currently send on to higher education and professional training a higher proportion of their school leavers than grammar schools ever did. Arguably, therefore, one of the things that grammar schools did not do was to infuse their pupils with an unquenchable thirst for more education. Other factors, and other institutions, have changed as much as schools in the last thirty years (among them an increase in the numbers of places available in higher education and a marked change in the culture of the middle class about the 'value' – particularly the economic value – of a higher education). These changes account, to a significant extent, for some of the increase in the number of young people in higher education. Going to university has, in the last three decades, become part of the common culture of a section of the middle class which would not previously have entertained the idea.

Thus what we have in the recent history of education is a curious situation. Those golden days of tripartite education did not in fact produce the students anxious to continue their experience of education. On the contrary, the despised comprehensives have become the institutions from which a large section of the undergraduate population outside Oxbridge is now drawn. The perception of this change in both political and academic circles is contradictory. On the one hand, the socially progressive praise the extension of the privileges of higher education to a wider section of the population while, from another point of view, the more-means-worse lobby express the vociferous opinion that today the standard of undergraduates entering universities is lower than in the past. The skill that is generally identified as lacking in the new generation is that of organised literacy – the ability to write essays in the classic grammar school mode of beginning, middle and end. The conventional sandwich essay so beloved of grammar school teachers was borrowed from the practices of elementary science: begin with a proposition to examine, examine it and then reach a conclusion. This method of organising knowledge was deemed satisfactory for everything from learning that hydrogen and oxygen would, if combined in the correct proportions, make water to agreeing that the French Revolution had a number of causes.

Learning to be proficient in this organisational skill was part and parcel of what a grammar school education was all about. To have an essay returned as 'badly organised' was the greatest shame. Such a commitment to rigorously narrative skill and style thus dominated the way in which thought was to be presented for public consumption. Even if an audience of middle-class children had come across such classics of children's literature as *Alice in Wonderland*, in which time and experience do not adhere to an orderly sequence, this was not to be the case at school. Here every exercise was to proceed along a model of the properly organised day: our task for today is this, and this is the way that we shall proceed to reach our stated objective. Since the school was a collective body, each individual was supposed to proceed at the ordained pace and both 'keeping up with the class' and 'not falling behind with the work' were frequently made rallying cries to the faint-hearted.

This particular instance of the practices of a conventional

grammar school is just one of the many practices that might be cited to support the case that grammar schools did not encourage participation in education, and that as much as being alien to the working class (a subject on which there is an extensive sociological literature) the culture of the conventionally organised grammar school was also alien, and alienating, to the middle-class child. It is a commonplace assumption of the sociology of education that it is the working-class child (or indeed girls and members of ethnic minorities) who are alienated by the experience of British secondary education. My suggestion here is that while these sections of the population may find secondary schools strange and/or hostile environments, so too do many middle-class children. The capacity of schools to alienate children continues therefore as a marked feature of all Western cultures, and memories of the past, sighs for a golden age, only serve to obscure the essential problem about schools: that their organisation, whether that of a traditional grammar school or a contemporary comprehensive, contains a number of features that increase the likelihood of a child, of whatever sex and from whatever background, becoming uninterested in the possibilities, in the most general sense, of education. To their endless credit the authors of one of the classic studies in the English sociology of education, Brian Jackson and Dennis Marsden, in *Education and the Working Class*, recognised the possible effects of conventionally organised schools when they wrote: 'Sometimes it was as if education was simply a package, to be considered, weighed and bought.'[1] And they go on to quote from F.R. Leavis that the 'conscious and intelligent incompleteness which carries with it the principle of growth' was generally absent. *Education and the Working Class* is often read as an attack on the way in which grammar schools excluded working-class pupils. That is certainly a part of Jackson and Marsden's argument. But a more radical strand to their argument is their assertion that the grammar school equated its own culture with that of culture *per se*. What Jackson and Marsden identify as the restrictive, closed culture of the grammar school was such as to be hostile to any genuine pursuit of educational excellence.

To make this argument Jackson and Marsden use a variety of sources. Lengthy quotations from Matthew Arnold and evidence that asserts the particular values of working-class life are introduced in a way that parallels passages in Richard Hoggart's *The Uses of Literacy*. What emerges from this original combination of ideas is an appeal that schools should not equate middle-class habits, expectations and aspirations with a culture that is in some sense real or absolute, let alone valuable. Learning middle-class deportment, Jackson and Marsden point out, is not the same as education. Probably many people involved in teaching children would agree with that sentiment. Yet what that assertion – correct enough in its general sense – also does is to contain two confusing, and politically significant, assumptions. In the first place the authors assume that grammar schools were well suited to middle-class children. Second, the authors assume a common middle-class culture – a culture that is apparently quite distinctive and different from that of the working class, not to mention the upper class. What both these assumptions do is to overemphasise both the homogeneity and the respect for education of the English middle class.

The political motives for attacking the grammar schools in the 1950s and 1960s may well have been impeccable. Faced with the massive evidence that demonstrated a conspicuous absence of the working class from higher education, it was inevitable that progressive educationalists and social scientists should have sought to identify the structural limitations and constraints on working-class educational achievement. So the evil presence in the English system of secondary education was the apparently middle-class culture of the grammar school. This alienating and all-pervasive force translated what should have been an education for all into an education for those with the existing cultural habits and tastes that enabled them to benefit from it.

Thus the cover of the Penguin edition of *Education and the Working Class* suggests to the reader, even before they have opened the book, that the working-class child is never going to make the transformation into the middle-class figure, fully equipped with blazer, cap and satchel. One child has the faint – very faint – air of a nascent James Dean, while the other (his mouth firmly shut and hair appropriately short) stands almost to attention. Body language had yet to be recognised in 1966 but clearly the stance of the two children suggests quite different attitudes to authority and order. We are asked, I think quite explicitly invited, to believe that the order of the grammar school can be normal and natural to the middle-class child and quite foreign and unnatural to the working-class child. The demolition of such formal rules and regulations of school life in the late 1960s and 1970s as the wearing of uniform and almost universal mandatory attendance at an unashamed Anglican school assembly both point to attempts, throughout secondary education, to come to terms with the world outside the school and to integrate into school life the life of the adolescent peer group. All these changes have been endlessly contentious, and any attempts by schools to raise the issues of sexism and racism in education are likely to be met with hostility and denial of the issue. However, despite these changes the numbers of working-class children who leave school with no formal qualifications still remains considerably higher than for their middle-class contemporaries.

The liberalisation of secondary education did not, of course, come about entirely as a result of the progressive spirit. What was also involved was bowing to the inevitable. The process of accepting the *force majeur* of the consumer society's youth culture was one which was rationalised in different ways. At one end of a continuum head teachers simply accepted what they could no longer control or police, at the other extreme, head teachers argued that schools had to take a lead in interpreting this new culture. Or, to put it another way, head teachers continued to claim their traditional power of interpreting the world. In whatever way, and for whatever reasons, the liberalisation of the secondary school came about, it was viewed with distaste in many quarters. The right attacked the decline of the authority of the school and the lowering of standards, while the left decried the continued evidence of working-class underachievement in education, which suggested that the middle-class culture of the school did not have quite so much to do with grammar schools *per se* as was once supposed. Indeed, the suspicion was increasingly voiced that academically gifted working-class children were more likely to do badly in comprehensive schools than in traditional grammar schools. This argument suggested that the new, liberal comprehensive school legitimated, in a way that grammar schools had not, the anti-intellectualism of aspects of a working-class environment.

Thus in the 1990s we arrive at the spectacle of a Conservative government attempting to revive educational practices and structures that had been written off as part of educational practice. The possible revival of selection at age eleven, the apparent appeal of more 'traditional' methods of teaching and appraisal all call for approval from the collective memory bank. And that collective memory bank draws part of its assessment of what schools ought to be like from a memory of the supposed academic and social coherence of English grammar schools in the 1950s and 1960s.

In these schools, it is argued, pupils were taught 'real facts' and taught in a way that produced people with skills that were immediately adaptable and transferable to the adult world. To demonstrate their case, conservatives have seized on what they perceive as the unacceptable shift in the practice of teaching certain subjects. The subject mentioned more than any other is that of history. The case made by Mrs Thatcher and her ministers is that abandoning the chronological teaching of history carries with it the cost of failing to teach children about continuity in the past. The problem of the nature of this continuity (that, as Samuel Beckett once said, 'time passes anyway') is obscured in a stream of stories about contemporary schoolchildren who cannot place in chronological order the Battles of Hastings and Trafalgar. The force of the anecdotal in politics is recognised by politicians of all persuasions; what clearly resonates for many parents is Mrs Thatcher's equation of memories of a shared scholastic experience with social cohesion and order. That the memory is misleading is an essential part of the argument of this book. But as well as casting doubts on Conservative, and conservative, memories of the past – which it is always easy enough to do – I also wish to examine some of the thinking which led the Left, or the 'progressives', to attack grammar schools. Elements of my dissatisfaction with that attack have already been hinted at in the brief discussion above of Jackson and Marsden. In these chapters I shall spell out more fully the particular elements of my argument that certain of the accusations levelled against grammar schools were misleading and often incorrect in their identification of the essential target.

Important as grammar schools were in maintaining social order, they seem to me to have been equally important in maintaining ideological order.

Let me begin, therefore, with my recollection of attending a grammar school in the late 1950s and the early 1960s. Almost the last years of educational peace, years in which pupils were still sufficiently intimidated by the authority of their teachers to believe that school rules had the force of absolute law and that there was some good reason for accepting the particular organisational eccentricities of the school. On the whole the school rules and regulations were accepted and obeyed. We wore the school uniform correctly, stayed within the school grounds all day, arrived there on time, and, in a variety of ways, from the mundane to the almost metaphysical, did not question the career and the life plan outlined for us. This life plan stated that until pupils had taken their O levels they would be supervised for every minute of the day and bring to school (and introduce into school work) only those texts and subjects provided by the school. This ideologically sealed world was allowed to crack a little in the sixth form; university entrance, and particularly university admissions interviews, demanded that pupils should have at least some basic information about the world outside. Hence the weekly civics classes with the Headmistress: in these exchanges we would try out on each other the sensible and informed answers on such immediately relevant topics as the super-power confrontation on Cuba and the political implications of the assassination of President Kennedy. To these classes we were allowed to bring daily newspapers and weekly magazines; otherwise such publications were proscribed reading. It was correctly recognised that while *The Times* or the *Manchester Guardian* were eminently respectable, they were also the thin end of a wedge which led to much less acceptable magazines. It is extraordinary to recall that in a completely ordinary grammar school in the English home counties in the early 1960s pupils actually had to hide from the eyes of authority copies of the *New Statesman* and the first of the Beatles' LPs.

In those days, this recollection suggests, some hard and fast lines were drawn between the acceptable and the unacceptable. Here, perhaps, lies part of the appeal of the grammar school

9

(and the continuing appeal of the public school). The appeal is that the school drew, and draws, lines between itself and the outside world which are particularly appealing to those who wish to identify a class-based, gendered identity. (Because the majority of girls' grammar and public schools so extensively and shamelessly aped the behaviour of the boys' schools it is not, I think, true to say that the traditional girls' grammar school contributed, in a straightforward way, to the creation of a gendered identity. On the contrary, girls' grammar schools and public schools probably confused the issue of gender identity more thoroughly than is generally supposed.) The wearing of uniform, the making of rules, the development of rivalries within the school in addition to those with other schools were all designed to foster a sense of identity and a sense of community that is singularly appropriate to the workplace or the community association. The primitive sense of 'us' and 'them' fostered by the grammar and public school has traditionally contributed to the particular culture of the English. The loss of the label 'grammar school' boy or girl therefore removes from the middle class a part of the process of social labelling that was largely taken for granted.

But successfully acquiring the label 'grammar school pupil' was always more problematic than is sometimes supposed, just as educational success is not a matter of entirely straightforward achievement. The strength of the hostility of conservatives to the abolition of the grammar school lies, perhaps, in the contradictory attitude of the English middle class towards individualism, and invidividual competition and achievement. On the one hand, the ethic is all for individual achievement, on the other, it is deeply suspicious of individual achievement that smacks of, or seems to arise from, nonconformity. Grammar schools often contained and lived out this contradiction: they were all about achievement (in that a pupil had to be demonstrably better than other pupils to be there in the first place) and yet had an uneasy relationship with individuals, or institutions, where those values of achievement and competition were most marked. Our civics classes were weekly exercises in being taught that individuals were not allowed to act merely for themselves. For example, in those far-off days a favourite question on scholarship level papers was 'What is a great leader?' and much attention was devoted to answering this question. The instinctive – and literal – answer – that a great leader is anyone who can get their own way and get other people to believe it – was never allowed. In its place we were encouraged to believe – and write – that a great leader was one who acted for the 'public good' and always acted mercifully and with proper respect for his or her enemies. Churchill was in, Hitler and Attila the Hun were out. Certain aspects of historical fact and other elements in our education were therefore overlooked; for example, the reasonably successful job that Hitler did, for at least some of the time, in convincing quite a lot of people that he was right.

So we were supposed to compete, and competition in the school was organised so that it occurred in a labyrinth of different ways. We were expected to compete with each other and to this end we were streamed, even before we actually set foot in the school, into A, B and C streams. We were not tested or evaluated by the school, the streaming was based entirely on our eleven plus results. Moreover, there was no liberal nonsense about A, B or C 'just' being letters of the alphabet: the A stream knew it was the A stream as surely as the C stream knew its own place in the world. In terms of the internal hierarchy of the school this streaming was further reinforced by the allocation to the A stream of teachers who were known to be heads of department or senior staff or teachers of subjects the school regarded as important. The first year C stream thus had as its form teacher a notably incompetent teacher of domestic science, while their contemporaries in the A stream were greeted each morning by the ex-Oxford Head of English. This complete segregation of pupils and staff continued throughout the first five years at the school – a degree of anarchy set in in the sixth form, but largely because it was only the A stream and sections of the B stream that survived that long. In my final year at the school a new Headmistress was appointed to the school. A graduate not of Oxbridge but of London she began to institute some tentative measures of reform. Among the first of these was the ending of automatic streaming for the first form entry, classes were now to be named merely after the surname of the class teacher. This modest reform was greeted with howls of outrage by the parents and a special meeting had to be held to explain that educational practice was moving towards both a greater scepticism of the eleven plus as an indicator of educational ability and the merits of early streaming.

However, the early years of our brilliant careers were lived out in the worlds of A, B and C. Within these classes we were subdivided for certain subjects – the guide to this practice was that the more important the subject, the more likely it was that the class would be divided so that the more able pupils were taught by senior staff. Thus the pupils were located in competitive terms from their earliest days in the school. So too were the subjects. On the one hand were the 'serious' subjects: English Literature, Classics, Modern Languages, Mathematics and the Sciences, Geography and History. On the other hand were Domestic Science, Religious Knowledge, Art, Games and Gymnastics and Music. All these latter subjects, from my admittedly subjective memory, were appallingly badly taught. In Music we sang one song for one term and heard Grieg's *Peer Gynt* so often I have completely suppressed all memory of it. Domestic Science was only required, for some pupils, for one year and on the joyous day when we could abandon Domestic Science for Classics we left behind half-smocked aprons which were to protect us against the cooking that we never did. As grammar school girls we rejected, if not compulsive heterosexuality, then certainly compulsory femininity. Cooking pineapple upside down cake had no place in our view of our futures and it was with delight that we left behind the curious world of making clothes and strange puddings. As children of our time, as much as products of our educational background, we also half-recognised that making clothes and cooking puddings were not skills that had a great deal of either social or economic value. Very plainly, we recognised and endorsed the cash nexus and the limited social value of the traditional work of women.

So the streams of the school passed their days in their appropriate tasks: Latin for the A stream, German for the B stream and Domestic Science and Spanish for the C stream. In the hierarchy of languages the Greeks and the Romans came off as the superior beings, the Germans as moderately academically respectable and the Spaniards, by implication, making do with a

12

language fit only for waiters and the dull-witted. To be assured of high academic honour within the school the subjects to excel at were English Literature and History. Being good at science and mathematics had no great social cachet or appeal. The school was entirely typical of the values of the English educational system in its scant regard for science and mathematics: these were subjects in which no literacy was involved, no individual intervention in the language of excellence. Like almost every girls' grammar or public school of its time, the school attached academic importance firmly and squarely to traditional arts subjects and failed to encourage or develop skills of numeracy and experimentation. The contemporary view is, of course, that this attitude and practice has now changed. Yet a cursory glance at the numbers of women either reading or teaching science or mathematics in British universities suggests that although the ideology about this situation may have changed, so that the under-representation of women in science is now seen as a 'bad' thing, the practices of schools have not. Several years ago the expression 'maths anxiety' became current in the United States to describe the reluctance of women to be taught, or want to be taught, mathematics. What is curious about the expression is that it suggests, as is all too ofen the case, that it is the pupils' fault (in this instance women's fault) if they find mathematics boring and uninteresting. Little is said about the teaching of the subject, let alone the subject itself, which demands a radical break in thinking to appreciate.

But radical breaks in thinking were not part of our education. Nobody suggested that in order to understand science or mathematics we had to abandon the accumulative and chronological model of learning that was the *sine qua non* of all the school's activities. The enforced educational career of the grammar school was one, therefore, which was not just hierarchical – in the sense of its rigid organisation of academic ability and academic importance – but rigidly chronological. Analysis, speculation and abstraction, the habits and characteristics of mind that might lend themselves to an interest in geometry or physics, were not part of the pattern of learning. Thus among the many things that the school never told us was that the nature of a mathematical problem was not the same *kind* of problem as assessing the competence of Keats as a poet of nature. Sitting in an endless fog of incomprehension and boredom, and surrounded by contemporaries who were equally bemused and bored, I joined in the eternal Greek chorus of the mathematics lesson: what is this all about? Our collective failure of imagination may have been our particular fault, but if so it was a failure that has been shared by generations of schoolgirls. My own recollection of mathematics is that unlike the subjects I enjoyed it led from the bad to the worse: understand one triangle and you were presented with another, more baffling, one. In History and English Literature our rewards were different. We progressed out of the dark ages of the feudal system, the complexities of the Elizabethan House of Commons and Chaucer to the heady and fascinating heights of industrialisation and the nineteenth-century novel. At last, in the Factory Acts and *Middlemarch* we could engage with subjects and issues that had some apparent relationship to reality.

Attempting to analyse what engaged me, and others, about these subjects involves identifying both the nature of particular academic subjects and the ways that they are generally taught. It is possible to state with some confidence that then, as now, the appeal of teaching as a career in certain subjects has always been greater in some cases than others. Graduates of arts subjects have fewer professional options open to them than those graduating in the sciences or mathematics. So in theory we should have been taught science and mathematics by people who specifically wanted to teach. Yet my recollection is that this was not, at least noticeably, the case. The individual staff cannot, of course, be held responsible for our massive exodus from the sciences at the first possible moment. (The moment was then – as now – immediately after O level.) Which leaves us with the subjects themselves, and the possibility that there is something so alien about mathematics and science that they can lose pupils almost on first encounter.

While this hypothesis is reassuringly familiar, it is in this context entirely inadequate. Thus I wish to suggest that what so alienated pupils from these subjects was part of the culture of the school itself. The school endorsed to the full the view that a proper education was an education based entirely in the liberal arts subjects. If these subjects could not be classics, then the next best thing was English Literature and History. What was singularly attractive about these subjects was that they lent themselves to two central themes in English bourgeois liberalism: the notion of progress in human history and the notion of the constant vitality and ingenuity of the English. The study of English Literature was thus a central vehicle for the development of a particular kind of understanding of the social and emotional world. The values of bourgeois culture have, since the sixteenth century, emphasised the importance of responsible individualism. To this end the novels of Austen, Eliot, Dickens et al. provide endless grist to the mill of a certain moral understanding of the world. We had all been taught, since we were children in primary school, that we had to care for others but also learn to look after ourselves and to do our best. Concern for others was interpreted and articulated in terms of codes of manners, models of behaviour and a certain respectful attitude to authority. We learnt these values through the pages of Beatrix Potter and later J.M. Barrie and Lewis Carroll. From the sad saga of the fierce bad rabbit and his insatiable greed for other rabbits' carrots it was a short conceptual step to the unhappy tale of Macbeth. Greed for possessions was universally condemned even in the same lessons which discussed the history of British imperialism. We learnt to condemn Macbeth and yet the Shakespearian history plays were our first formally approved lessons in straightforward nationalism.

But we fought the French, in the fourteenth and the fifteenth centuries, for the same reasons that we fought the Germans in the twentieth century – because the British had right on their side and were the champions, throughout their history, of good against evil. History, therefore, came easily to children of a culture which had already inculcated belief in the superiority of the British and the benefits of British influence. There were, of course, hiccups on the path of true righteousness, but these hiccups in the historical unfolding of the British genius were rapidly accounted for by individual mistakes, by individuals who had insufficiently integrated an understanding of proper behaviour. Alternatively, individuals were, like poor George III, just mad. Fortunately, no sooner had a mad, bad monarch departed from the scene (such as George III or the Prince Regent) than a good and sensible person, be it Queen Victoria or Pitt, came along to sort things out. The British were always saved. Whether from aristocratic despotism, the French threat or the shadow of the jackboot, someone always turned up to rescue us from the unhappy and/or dangerous state into which we were about to fall.

Enshrined in these historical lessons was a belief in the justice of British actions. We were not being exploitative in our imperialism (unlike of course the French, the Spanish and the Germans) and the central values of entrepreneurial capitalism, aggressive accumulation and the centrality of property rights, were assumed uncritically in our seven-year voyage of historical discovery from the Stone Age to the First World War. The wars, both civil and national, that occurred in this saga (and a saga that led to the heady uplands of the late twentieth-century cold war) occurred because of other people's immoral actions or failures of reason. The most frequent form of immorality in international events and international history was that of greed — greed for possessions and greed for political control were the two failings that brought about the collapse of empires or their decay and destruction. This version of history as a moral saga may well have changed in that it is nowadays virtually imposs-ible not to include questions of the material world and material acquisition in historical discussions. But from the evidence of the version of history of the contemporary Right on both sides of the Atlantic (not to mention the more local example of the views of the world of first-year undergraduates) what is still being taught is that the desire to accumulate property is a natural part of the human condition. And not only is it a natural part, it is a 'good' part, in that it is only through this spirit of acquisitiveness that the engine of history, and historical change, is fired into action. The idea has recently been mooted that British universities and schools should instruct their students in the 'enterprise culture'. The idea, presumably, is that students should be taught that private property, private accumulation and private enterprise are synonymous with the good life. Indeed, in *The Times* of 18 February 1988, Kenneth Baker was quoted as saying that he hoped that schools would soon return to more 'rigour in their teaching and a greater emphasis, in the best Victorian sense, on the values of discipline'.

This conservative view of the Victorians has been attacked and deconstructed so many times that I do not wish to revive the debate. Suffice to say here that the view is entirely selective and largely a code for saying that in the nineteeth century mechanisms of social control were, in some instances, more easily guaranteed. Children did sit in rows in school, they did accept the discipline of the school and they were taught a range of subjects, and an interpretation of those subjects, so narrow as to be almost unrecognisable in the modern context. Yet Kenneth Baker and like-minded Ministers hail these days as the departed golden age; in his remarks in the press while Secretary of State for Education, Kenneth Baker made much of the glories of past education. One of its great strengths – and a particularly popular one with other nostalgic writers on education – was its emphasis on grammar. Grammar, again to quote Kenneth Baker, is one of the cornerstones of education.

And back in the great days of the grammar school we learnt grammar. Not only did we learn the grammar of our own language, we learnt other people's languages through their grammar. We sat and analysed sentences in terms of their grammatical structure. We underlined verbs in green, nouns in red, adverbs in hyphenated green and adjectives in hyphenated red. There were other colours for other actors in the theatre of grammar, but clearly they had such a minor role in the literary construction of life that they have long since slipped from my memory. The years of elaborate colour coding of my thoughts left me – and I suspect most of my contemporaries – with a distant memory that grammar is rather like traffic lights – if it's a verb it goes, if it's a noun it roots you to the spot. The inhibitions of learning to write English in this way were probably not decisively inhibiting for most of us, in that outside the school we had the free space to write letters or other compositions in our native tongue that could be as ungrammatical as we cared to make them. The truly inhibiting effect was in learning other people's languages. Confronted by real-life French or Germans or Spanish we were collectively confounded by the ability of these people to speak in tongues that we had only read about.

Nor was this culture shock confined to a foreign land; within our own culture the speech of groups and regions outside standard middle-class English was as foreign as that of the inhabitants of Paris or Madrid. When English new wave cinema began to vie for a place in the culture of the 1950s and early 1960s we were warned against such films as *Saturday Night and Sunday Morning* on the grounds that these films could severely damage our grammar. When we received grudging permission in the sixth form to read *Look Back in Anger*, the analysis of some of the more extensive diatribes of Jimmy Porter was in terms less of their content than of their grammar. Others in my generation recognised much more clearly than we did the colossal confidence trick of much of the way that English was taught in schools. In the *Beyond the Fringe* parody of Shakespeare ('get thee to Lancaster, Kent, and thee York to Canterbury' and so on) there lay the recognition that what was being taught was a code, and a code designed for purposes of social recognition as much as those of education and the advancement of literature.

The dislike and distaste of the way in which I, and millions of others, were taught the central liberal disciplines of British culture is not in any sense either a unique nor particularly unhappy memory. An extensive section of English autobiography deals with dislike of school. From Orwell's fierce indictment of his prep school in *Such, Such were the Joys* to the more measured condemnations of Graham Greene, not being happy at school, and being suspicious of its curriculum, are frequent subjects of reminiscence. But most of the accounts are by men, educated at public school and later to be successful in ways which were in some sense unorthodox. And even the famous accounts of being unhappy at school – like that of Orwell – have to be qualified by other comments. Cyril Connolly, who attended the same prep school as Orwell, claimed that he himself was not unhappy there. Moreover, Orwell, although he loathed the infamous St Cyprian's, seems to have enjoyed Eton. As Bernard Crick writes of the school and Orwell's relationship to it:

All in all, however, if his career at Eton had been unsuccessful by College standards, he had got a lot out of it, in terms of reading and self-confidence. And he had not been unhappy; he had simply stood aside from official enthusiasm and had, indeed, flexed his muscles in practical scepticism of authority.[2]

I quote this passage and cite this example because it suggests, I think, one of the central features of a supremely self-confident school and the contrast that this can provide to the less confident, and hence more authoritarian and rigid school. This is not to suggest that all public schools have the self-confidence to allow nonconformity and degrees of individual creativity – clearly they do not and, again, a considerable literature demonstrates the collective anxiety of many a public school. But what it does suggest is that the expectations imposed on schools – by anxious parents paying fees that they can barely afford, or by suspicious local education authorities or reactionary governments – are reflected in the internal organisation of schools. To many parents, and voters, grammar schools looked as if they knew what they were doing simply because they existed in a state-imposed system of selection at eleven plus and in a period in which codes of dress and behaviour were, at least for the middle class, relatively uniform and rigid, at least in their superficial appearance. Yet – and this remains the central argument of this essay – in reality the school had very little idea of what it wanted to teach, or why, and the daily worship of order and hierarchy played a central part in occupying a normative vacuum. The particular character of this vacuum was: first, an uneasy relationship between ideas of femininity and ideas of academic excellence; second, an uncertain understanding of academic excellence; and third, a troubled and somewhat incoherent view of the relationship between the possible coherence and achievements of the academic and intellectual worlds and the social order of Britain in the late twentieth century.

The first of these problems is particular, of course, to all girls' schools, although there is arguably a case to be made for the existence of an unease about masculinity as traditionally and conventionally conceived and the intellectual and creative aspirations of certain liberal arts subjects. Affectivity in men, as generations of social psychologists and sociologists have observed, is a problem for cultures with particularly authoritarian, and segregated, views of masculinity. So all the three disjunctions mentioned above can, I would argue, be found throughout the English school system. And it was a disjunction which led to the reforms of the 1960s and the 1970s: reforms which have now been challenged and are leading to the attempts of the present government to achieve a perfect 'fit' between schools and the social values which it endorses. It is, however, the precise nature of the disjunctions mentioned above that I wish to explore briefly here.

The uneasy relationship between conventional ideas of femininity and the academic achievements of women is now widely acknowledged. There are shelves of books about the battle that women fought to enter higher education. White, middle-class women who went to school and university in the 1950s were taught by women who had had to fight this battle and had been educated as exceptions. This much has now changed. But even if there are more women graduates and more women in teaching, the central question that dogged women's education still remains: what exactly is women's education for? There are endless liberal answers of the kind that are the major material for speech days and degree ceremonies, but there is also the constant problem of the existence of a world outside the school in which the sexual division of labour – both in and outside the household – maintains an unbroken relationship between women and the care and service of others. If a past generation chose not to follow the role model of spinster school-teachers (all of whom in my recollection lived to a spry and great old age) then a present generation may find it equally unattractive to follow the example of married women teachers, working a double shift. Structural constraints on women aside, there remains the more complex issue of femininity and the school. Heterosexuality is now the accepted sexual reality of the school, and within that context adolescent girls are supposed to learn the skill of both the accepting and rejecting of men. Sex in school, as the headlines might say, is the subject of a later chapter. Suffice to say here that the ideology of achievement presented girls' schools with academic aspirations which involved encouraging masculine, and masculinist, habits of intellectual self-assertion and rational thinking. Virginia Woolf was among the many women who noticed the material discrepancies of men's and women's education. The prunes and claret contrast of women's colleges and men's colleges is a much cited argument of *A Room of One's Own*. Yet more important is the point she develops later in the essay – that, in her view, the creative power of women 'differs greatly from the creative power of men'. And she asks the question that is still relevant: 'Ought not education to bring out and fortify the differences rather than the similarities?'[3] The problem, of course, is deciding what the differences and similarities are; defining masculinity and femininity has confounded many people and there remains considerable scepticism about adopting definitions that may in themselves be repressive.

The second problem for schools, then as now, is exactly what constitutes academic excellence – what should schools encourage as 'good'? In the 1950s the answer was straightforward: 'well-written', grammatical essays which made the conventional points and even, occasionally, made original points. From the outside, our school books, like those of our Victorian predecessors, looked correct. Order and grammar are easy enough to learn and they are a recognisable product, the 'formal' learning that Basil Bernstein has identified as distinct from more amorphous, and certainly less immediately measurable, 'informal' learning. The appeal of those grammar school habits to conservative educational policy-makers is that there, in neat script, is what looks like a useful tool that can be put to useful work. The problem – that of academic and intellectual excellence – might be defined as the problem of *Ulysses* – or, to put it in a way more familiar to schoolchildren, the problem of *Jane Eyre*. In the first instance we have Joyce writing a highly ungrammatical novel, with no punctuation, no apparently well-organised beginning and no well-organised middle or conclusion. In fact, the whole thing would fail O level English Language. Equally, try as GCE examiners might, it is difficult to disguise the fact that *Jane Eyre* is a novel about the rejection of convention, not to mention authority in school. Those Victorian critics who condemned the novel as radical and dangerous could recognise social dissent when they saw it: here was a woman asserting a right to an autonomous judgment of the social and moral world. Both these novels are regarded as classics of English literature, yet they arise out of traditions and values that question authority and reject conventional habits and ways of life.

So exactly what is academically and intellectually excellent? And how, in schools occupying not the dizzy and supremely self-confident social heights of Eton, but the middle ground of professional toil and prescribed horizons, could pupils be taught to be good at school and good for a particular kind of life? Thus the third issue for schools, and the issue that haunts them to this day: how to convey the right kind of order for the world in which the pupils are going to live. The emphasis on order in grammar schools was, I would argue, an emphasis on precisely that. What the school was not about was coherence in any sense of putting together different issues and problems. Its strength was in teaching skills of the orderly presentation of agreed problems and arguments, with a certain licence for occasional individualism. Academic achievement was never allowed to be everything (hence the universal dislike of the swot and the equally universal award of the school prize to the good 'all rounder'). Even if honour boards listed the names of the pupils who went on to university, other internal institutions of the school existed to debunk and deflate the excessively intellectual. Well-mannered, academically competent semi-philistinism provided the identikit features of the perfect pupil.

Confronting the school as an institution while a pupil was inevitably an experience in which reflection on the educational making of the British national culture was limited. Reading about schools some twenty years after leaving them provided some interesting insights, not least into the assumption by sociologists that people have little idea what they are doing. I remember laughing out loud at first discovering the term 'hidden agenda' in the context of sociological discussions of schools. What I remember about school was the complete openness of the agenda sociologists described as 'hidden', a quite explicit agenda in which social values and moral assumptions were as much a part of the fabric of everyday life as the smell of the classrooms and the endless collection of old shoes in the cloakroom. From table manners to the relative social standing of different British universities a moral and social world was laid out for our consumption and our acceptance. The very considerable literary achievements of the British bourgeoisie and petit-bourgeoisie were presented to us in this context, and perhaps because of British theoretical incoherence in politics and philosophy, became the texts by which moral and political understanding was to be formed. Thus misunderstanding the British realist novel was – and is – such a central part of British secondary education. In the *Sunday Times* of 28 February 1988, Kenneth Baker aired more of his views on schools – on this occasion to encourage pupils to read more. So far, so good. But what he wants them to read, and why, is another matter. An implicit assumption of his article is that the nineteenth-century British novel is a kind of consumer's guide to life – an experience from which a pupil cannot but emerge with the proper understanding of bourgeois society. 'Back to the text' thus becomes a kind of educational fundamentalism – very cheap and likely to lead to the proper political conclusion of the individual who 'earns' a successful life.

And so what we were supposed to learn – and what took years to unlearn – was that human history was formed by some all-powerful force, in which individuals could only play their part by doing their best. The individual as the *active* subject of history was totally absent. Doing their best meant following the correct rules and making sensible choices. These rules and choices were constructed for the common good. Real enthusiasms for teaching, for learning, were tempered – and in the case of some individuals destroyed – by a culture designed for order. But it was an order born out of a hard-won battle for education, a battle in which women in particular had had to take on both the class and the gender characteristics of their antagonists. To be a successful grammar school girl involved, therefore, absorbing two specific (but conflicting) identities. First, that of the androgynous middle-class person who is academically successful in an academic world that is apparently gender blind. Second, that of the well-behaved middle-class woman who knows how to defer to and respect the authority of men.

2

Culture and Class

Being a grammar school pupil has always had status in English society – any grammar school, however inferior or unsuccessful, has been able to make to the world the proud boast that its pupils have been 'selected'. This has meant, of course, that they have passed the selective eleven plus examination and have chosen to opt for this particular kind of education. Passing the eleven plus was thus a major event in a child's life: if you passed you had access to the school where pupils wear uniform, take publicly recognised examinations and stay on at school until late adolescence. Not passing – at least in the 1950s – meant going to the school with no uniform, no examinations and a short career. At fifteen, from secondary modern schools, generations of English children were released to the labour market with scarcely a qualification between them. The minimal, indeed virtually non-existent, academic or vocational achievements and qualifications of pupils from secondary modern schools thus constituted as much a motive for the reorganisation of English secondary education (and the abolition of the grammar schools) as any liberal concern about the academic selection and categorisation of children at the age of ten.

Inside the golden world of educational success the yellow brick road led from the eleven plus to GCE O and A level. Being good at exams, and being able to summon up the wit to perform well on these occasions, was a skill which the school fostered and rewarded. The culture of the school made much of being successful at examinations. Yet being good at examinations was a skill which in a sense challenged two of the school's other values: being a consistent, conscientious worker was not always the same as being good at examinations, and learning to do well at examinations involved learning some of the abilities (such as a ruthless capacity to distinguish the important from the unimportant fact) that challenged the authority of received wisdom. In this chapter, therefore, I want to explore the ways that we learnt, not just the serious contradictions and paradoxes in the process of learning, being taught and taking examinations, but also the language and culture of the divisions of the English class system.

For the great majority of English children in the 1950s and the 1960s the eleven plus was the first (and in many cases the last) public examination that they took. On one single day in the January of our last year in primary school we were marshalled into the gymnasium of a local secondary school and asked (no, told) to take three papers: in Mathematics, English Language and something called General Intelligence. The mathematics paper (and this was at least a decade before any sign of a 'new' mathematics) involved simple addition, subtraction and so on. My recollection is that this paper was simply dull. English language on the other hand involved greater creative possibilities: we were invited to write about a recent outing (bad luck if you had the misfortune not to go on them) and describe the happiest day of our holidays. These two exercises in the recollection of middle-class social life were accompanied by tests of word comprehension. (For readers born after these days this involved demonstrating that we knew what a dog was by underlining the word animal from a choice of flower, person and tea cup, or some other random collection of nouns. General Intelligence was about the recognition of order in the symbolic world: numbers and patterns in sequence was the test here and a mania for the orderly classification of the universe was a valuable skill.) All these papers lasted about half an hour, and so after one and a half hours the die was cast, our educational fate was sealed. In those days there was no assessment element in this testing; it was make or break on one day.

Passing or failing these tests was announced some three

months later. I remember that summer had almost come when a bleak postcard arrived which stated that I had passed the 'selective examination'. Bureaucrats did not use the term 'eleven plus' and so the educational segregation of the ten-year-old population was given the kind of ideological gloss that the term 're-settlement' gave to the forced deportation of the Jews in Nazi Germany. Indeed, the very term 'selection' suggested a lengthy process of careful thought by the selectors, rather than a cursory, and limited, test which gave middle-class children considerable advantages. Indeed, unless middle-class children could not do the most simple mathematics I suspect that the eleven plus was almost impossible to fail – or put it another way, the eleven plus was almost impossible for working-class children to pass. The emphasis on the written word, and a particular kind of Janet and John, petit-bourgeois normality that the tests relied on, demanded a conceptual leap that many children clearly found impossible to make. Added to this, the examination had different implications in different parts of the country and for boys and girls: the numbers of grammar school places were, for example, traditionally higher in Wales than in other parts of the country and throughout England the numbers of places available in grammar schools for girls were lower than for boys. All these points have since been extensively documented, and only recently Birmingham's education authority was found guilty of maintaining discriminatory practices by allocating more 'selective' places to boys than to girls.

So those of us 'selected' at the tender age of ten for admission to grammar schools could, with some justification, think of ourselves as particularly blessed. And how homogeneous we were. Arriving at grammar school on the first day of the first term, the most striking characteristic of the other new pupils was that they too arrived in cars, from detached homes and with standard English voices. Everybody was fully equipped with the expensive uniform, and everyone could be reliably expected to own books and pens. The sheer cost of passing the eleven plus was identified, rightly, in the 1950s as a disincentive to working-class children and their parents. The emotional and social cost of being plunged into a middle-class world was doubtless considerable, but equally significant for many homes must have been the capital outlay necessary to take part in this new educational experience. It is no exaggeration to say that we needed an entire new wardrobe: from socks to vests and knickers to skirts, hats (one for summer, one for winter), shoes (three pairs at the minimum, one for summer, one for winter and one for indoors), coat, scarf and gloves. The whole outfit was completed by that symbol of masculine, white-collar order: the tie. We were expected to be clad in entirely uniform navy blue, to be purchased at an eminently respectable department store in London. Since the school was some 40 miles from central London, just going to buy the clothes entailed expense. Nor was this list of everyday clothes the only list that our parents were presented with. In addition there was also the sports list (two pairs of shorts, an aertex shirt, plimsolls, hockey boots and a sporting sweater) and the list of semi-industrial training wear – that is, the overall for science, the pinafore for domestic science and the totally encompassing shroud for arts and crafts. This list is still incomplete: I have omitted the swimming costume, the swimming hat and the bags for shoes and books. When our mothers took out their cheque books to pay for this mountain of clothes they were buying into an educational world which was clearly going to differentiate between those who passed the eleven plus (and wore uniform) and those who did not. Inevitably, bright working-class children were excluded from a world which was expensive even before they had entered it.

Nevertheless, one or two working-class pupils did enter this select, and selected, world. Yet how they were expected to survive it, and not commit suicide in the playground, is a vivid, if retrospective question. Two practices of the school made class divisions and distinctions immediately apparent. During the first week at school we all had to complete forms giving our father's occupation (such were those days that a) fathers automatically had occupations, b) children automatically had resident fathers, and c) mothers were full-time mothers) and submit to a shoe inspection. The exercise of completing the form about our personal circumstances produced the inevitable parade of middle-class occupations: as doctor followed architect, solicitor, bank manager, teacher, civil servant, university teacher and so endlessly on and on, it was really bad luck, almost bad form, to interrupt this panorama of suburban life with a lone voice saying factory worker or merchant seaman. Those two occupations struck me at the time as part of a foreign and bizarre world. Where did those fathers work, we wondered? Since we were used to coming to school and passing the schools, the banks, the surgeries and the offices where our fathers worked – and which we assumed represented the world of work – it was something of a problem to find a physical location for a factory worker or a seaman. The town in which our grammar school was located was devoid of industry, light or heavy, and so it was immediately apparent that here, in our midst, were people from hitherto unexplored territories.

But if occupational uniformity was demonstrated by the answers to this form so too was domestic uniformity. In my year at school we did not have one child from anything approaching a 'broken' home: divorce had made no impact on the English middle classes (or for that matter any class) in the 1950s. What did constitute social deviance and marginality in those far-off days was largely constituted by two factors – having a mother with a job, and belonging to a religion other than Church of England. Anglicanism, in the 1950s, was not a form of social radicalism. Nor did two-career families constitute a suburban norm. Yet even these two factors were limited to a tiny number of pupils: one or two girls in each class had mothers who had jobs, and about a dozen in each year were either Roman Catholic or Jewish. Of these deviants the Jewish girls were the most immediately visible, since they had to stand outside the school hall each morning while the rest of us trooped in to share a Bible reading, a hymn (Songs of Praise version) and prayers. These prayers followed the reliable pattern of the Lord's Prayer, a prayer on the subject of moral qualities ('Oh God, make me humble, modest and kind' and never 'Please God, make me clever, rich and beautiful') and a prayer about great issues of the day. Since I attended grammar school between 1957 and 1964 we spent a great deal of our morning devotional energies in pleas to the Almighty to bring peace between the United States and the Soviet Union. In 1961 these prayers took a turn for the almost frantic as the super-powers confronted each other over Cuba and a considerable shadow of doubt was cast over the likelihood of the next away fixture for the hockey team. From these supplications the Jewish girls were excluded. They had to linger in the corridor as the massed battalions of the Church of England filed in.

No such visibility was given to girls with working mothers. The school anyway endorsed the view – later taken up by feminists and feminism – that every mother was a working mother. The responsibilities of the housewife and the mother were given full credit by the staff and 'making a home' was an ideal which was accorded full status by a staff that was largely unmarried. So having a 'working' mother was regarded as slightly peculiar, and rather eccentric, but not seriously threatening to the *status quo* as it was assumed that working mothers were simply women who chose to do a little bit more than others. They remained, therefore, part of the assumptive world of the school, as women who were primarily mothers but also had paid interests. When the school debated the issue that 'A Woman's Place is in the Home' the school decided that this was certainly the case. Women should be at home, waiting for us to come home and ready to ferry us about to dancing class or whatever else. If women did not do this, and accept this way of life, then their only alternative fate was to be an unmarried schoolmistress. In the late 1950s this career did not look attractive and the dichotomy between employed woman and wife and mother remained absolute.

So distinctions were made, and apparent, on the basis of our religions and our fathers' occupations. Distinctions were also made, and were equally rapidly apparent, on the basis of the shoes on our feet. At the beginning of our first term, and at the beginning of every subsequent term, we had to produce the regulation number of pairs of shoes and submit them to examination. To many readers this apparently trivial exercise may appear as precisely that, just an exercise in the endless pedantry that is possible when an institution decides on enforcing a uniform dress code. Equally, the exercise might sound like one of those very sensible nanny exercises that the English sometimes engage in. Making sure that we were wearing shoes that did not deform or harm our feet was, from the point of view of the

29

health-conscious, a perfectly justifiable exercise. But this shoe inspection had another aspect to it which made it an immediate indicator of social class: 'good' shoes, made by Clarks and Start-Rite, were the shoes of the middle class (and immediately passed as acceptable) whereas 'bad' shoes, sold in shops such as Bata and Freeman, Hardy and Willis, were held up for condemnation and dismissal. Thirty years ago English grammar schools had not moved to the more classless running shoe as the universal footwear of pupils, and the battle over shoes was fought at the beginning of each term. Passing shoe inspection meant wearing 'sensible' shoes which had flat heels and round toes. The arrival of the stiletto heel threw the school authorities into a state of mild panic. These shoes were quite specifically designed as fashion, and what's more, they made terrible holes in the parquet floors. School dances and parents' evenings were thus always accompanied by stern memoranda utterly condemning the wearing of these loathsome objects, and many a fashion-conscious sixth former or parent had to spend an evening walking around entirely shoe-less.

That part of the exercise may have been comic (as was the sight of older girls changing out of or into stiletto heels as soon as they passed through the school gates) but what was not so comic were the social distinctions made between individuals on the basis of what they had on their feet. 'Good' shoes cost more than cheap shoes, and actually having the three pairs of shoes that the school demanded was in itself a significant capital expenditure. So what was being examined in this ostensibly harmless exercise was, first, the financial resources of our parents. But the second aspect of us, and our homes, that was on trial in the parade was a set of moral attitudes about appearance and vanity. 'Good' girls did not bother about whether or not their shoes were fashionable. They chose shoes that were functional, good for their feet and as inconspicuous as possible. 'Bad' girls chose shoes that were flimsy, fashionable and as conspicuously part of an attempt at chic as was possible within the extremely narrow boundaries of school uniform. To care about one's appearance was therefore part of an unacceptable attitude to the world. This did not mean that any kind of careless attire would do; on the contrary, it meant that as far as possible a 'good' girl did not have an appearance. What she had was a correct uniform, which gave the world the correct message about her – that is, that she was a well-behaved, sensible person who could be trusted not to wish to attract attention to herself by an unusual, let alone a fasionable appearance.

This training in how to dress is quite obviously still an extremely successful one. Although many grammar schools have not only been abolished as institutions but have abolished school uniform as part of their new existence as comprehensive schools, a glance at any gathering of the British middle and upper classes shows that uniformity in dress is still deeply ingrained. From Clarks and Start-Rite shoes women progress almost automatically to Jaeger, Laura Ashley and Russell and Bromley while the working class progress equally inevitably to C&A and British Home Stores. Whatever the more bizarre choices of dress of younger members of the British Royal Family it remains consistently true that the wealthy, or even the comfortably off, like their clothes to suggest nothing other than a class uniform, in the way that our school uniforms once suggested a universal acceptance of a certain way of life and particular views of the world. Scorned by the values of this world were personal narcissism and an interest in style. These attitudes and inclinations were somehow vulgar and vaguely suggestive of an unhealthy preoccupation with self and sexual attraction.

So 'good' girls were expected to have little interest in clothes, no personal narcissism and no interest in self-expression in dress. In maintaining this expectation the school's position was similar to that of King Canute. Any generation of adolescent girls is preoccupied with its appearance; a generation growing up in the late 1950s and early 1960s, at the beginning of a youth culture and in the middle of a consumer boom, was obsessed by its appearance. But even in this obsession the effect of the class system was to make us aware of the complexities surrounding the matter of dress. A complete lack of interest in dress was quite uncommon among my contemporaries; what was much more common was a studied and affected apparent lack of interest that masked either a complete or near complete obsession. Admitting to caring about the matter was about the same as saying that you were in favour of sin. Since dress had been

31

defined as the preoccupation of the vulgar lower orders, to admit to a real, passionate and absorbing interest in the details of appearance was to identify with an alien part of the culture. Learning how to be attractive and yet not sexually provocative, neat and yet not uniform, and financially solvent without looking ostentatious was part of the delicate and tortuous business of learning a class identity. Slogans such as 'If you've got it, flaunt it' and the outrageous flamboyance of media stars were light years away from the carefully calculated combinations of matching skirts and jumpers.

The official view of the school was, of course, that the wearing of uniform would banish from our innocent heads all thoughts of the possibilities of dress. It was also assumed, equally incorrectly, that school uniform would banish any social distinctions between the pupils and produce a wonderfully homogeneous group of pupils, united by their allegiance to the school. All these views were incorrect. First, we exploited to the full the sartorial possibilities of the school uniform. These were not extensive, but in so far as we were able we modified our navy blue serge to take account of the fashions of the real world. Skirts were taken in at the waist and the waistbands endlessly rolled over to shorten the length. (In this way we could pass skirt inspection – 'all skirts must touch the floor when the wearer is kneeling' – and yet hitch up our skirts as soon as we were out of the school grounds.) The hated school hats were universally converted from a coal scuttle shape to the Breton style that we fondly believed would make us instantly resemble Audrey Hepburn in one of her more *ingénue* roles. Against this tide of battered felt and Panama hats the school fought a losing battle: parents were simply not prepared to pay for endless, expensive new hats and in the end the school had to accept that as long as we had something on our heads that vaguely resembled a school hat then no complaints would be made. Manipulating the school uniform into something resembling ordinary clothes was carried on with universal enthusiasm and those girls who succeeded in tapering their school blazers into snug-fitting jackets were regarded with awe.

Just as wearing school uniform did not stop us thinking about clothes, so wearing school uniforms did not diminish the differences and distinctions between us. Our shoes gave away middle-class incomes, and the other personal possessions that the school had somehow or other forgotten to specify also revealed the rich, the poor, the vulgar, the tasteful. School satchels, spectacles, wrist watches and all the other bits and pieces that we took with us to school demonstrated both the purchasing power of our parents and their taste. Just to own expensive goods was not in itself prestigious – the 'right' possessions were those that combined a degree of expense with a certain exclusivity or wit. For this reason, access to 'abroad' was a mark of real status: anything French had the immediate effect of sending us into the kind of haze of veneration that some of our parents obviously shared for 'anything French'. Francophilia has long been a feature of the educated English middle class and this small section of it was no exception. French clothes, French food, French anything were rated as inherently superior to their Anglo-Saxon equivalents. The actual reality of France, and its many lapses from high bourgeois taste, was not critically considered. (Nor did an enthusiasm for France carry with it an ability to speak French.) Yet in this attitude to France (and an accompanying lack of interest in other European cultures) lay a juvenile version of many English adult attitudes to abroad. We were fascinated by the possibilities of warm, sunny climates in the same way as were characters in E.M. Forster; the desire to travel (for quite unthought-out reasons) was part of our ambitions for the future and our definition of what was worth travelling to (France, Italy, Spain and India) corresponded exactly to the limits of the eighteenth- and nineteenth-century Grand Tour and the most obviously civilised of the ex-colonies. No one had the slightest interest in travelling to Africa, South America or Australasia. The United States remained largely foreign, a rather crass country glimpsed more or less entirely through the advertisements in the *National Geographic* magazine. In discussions about where we would travel to (if we all had the luck to be air hostesses when we grew up) it was generally agreed, and endorsed by the staff, that the United States would not be interesting as it 'had no history'.

So 'having no history' was a major qualification to be considered as a serious country. And 'having a history' did not mean having been there a long time, or with a culture that might well have gone back to the Stone Age. It meant having a written culture, which had produced great works of literature, imposing buildings, scientific and technological innovations and all the other artefacts that were so manifestly a part of nineteenth- and twentieth-century European bourgeois culture. This qualification, and these conditions, therefore brought together a curious combination of great cultures: the French, the Italians, the Germans and the Spanish were there, with the Greeks and Romans in a special, venerated position. But also included were the Egyptians, the Chinese and the Indians. Virtually everyone else was left out, and entirely left out were any countries of sub-Saharan Africa. It was a view which was inherently racist in its emphasis on white cultures but it was also a view which equated civilisation with cultural artefacts and progress towards (eventually) the good life of industrial society. Those African countries which were, in the 1950s, progressing slowly and painfully towards emancipation from colonialism were shadowy, and alarming, places on the world stage.

British civilisation and British qualities were nevertheless defined in contrast to these strange and uncivilised places. We were encouraged to worry about what was then called the 'underdeveloped' world, but it was a concern rooted in a very precise assertion of our difference and of our superiority. The world, in terms of different nations and different cultures, was thus a markedly hierarchical place, and it was this pervasive sense of the hierarchical arrangements of the social world (rather than a simple-minded racism as such) that structured our thinking and our assumptions. Every physical object, every social relationship, every human being had a particular place in a carefully evaluated world and learning this grading system was a fundamental part of our education. Hence the appeal, to conservatives, of schools that could so successfully inculcate into their pupils the proper, ordered perception of the world, a perception in which things, people and places were not just different, but better or worse. From how to dress to attitudes to abroad, we learnt what was right and what was suitable.

But for all the strength and consistency of the school's ability to impose a set of values and manners on its pupils it has to be said that it was working with a group that was already homogeneous and imbued with the major values and beliefs of the English middle class. We did not come to the school with our heads full of radical, subversive ideas that had to be translated by a painful educational process into coherent and consistent conservatism. If our heads were full of anything, they were full of the vague snapshots and slogans of middle-class infancy and childhood. We had learned not to speak to strangers, to be polite to adults, to play with some children and not others. Many of us, in those days before video films and a global childhood culture of space creatures and warlike beings, had learned our social relations through A.A. Milne and the Reverend Audry. Robert Louis Stevenson had invited us to rejoice in our Britishness; as he said, 'Little Turk or Japanese, / O! Don't you wish that you were me?' Put like that, the position of most of us did seem enviable. If only we worked hard, and continued to be good, then we would continue to enjoy the privileges of living in middle-class suburbia, surrounded by middle-class comfort and security.

Little wonder that this world remains such an evocative and appealing world for the English middle class, and equally little wonder that reproducing this world maintains such a persistent and potent appeal for voters and politicians alike. To guarantee a world in which children go to school in uniform, stay there all day, pass examinations and then become conscientious citizens is deeply attractive. Thus replicating this world, through reviving selection at age eleven, instituting compulsory, and frequent, evaluation and allowing (indeed encouraging) schools to opt out of the public sector altogether suggests a ruthless determination to re-establish both a set of values and a set of institutional practices that have, in conservative analyses, disappeared in a tide of meritocratic standards and moral pluralism. Those schools which do choose to opt out of the public system will, it is presumably hoped, go the way of council homes liberated from public ownership – they will rapidly become small fortresses of the ideal of private property, and generously glorified with the proper hallmarks (the neo-Georgian front door and the front porch, which helps to maintain a proper distinction between the public and the private) of a reverence for the successful, and acceptable, past and the existing distinctions of the social world.

Clearly, opted-out schools are, at least in the imagination of Conservative Ministers, the schools that will revive and revitalise proper traditions and useful values.

That most of these values have both not disappeared, and were never seriously challenged, is seldom allowed. The onslaught of the liberal 1960s, and the general liberalisation of institutional practice in secondary higher education, quite obviously affected the kind of rules and regulations that we lived under in the late 1950s and early 1960s. Pupils at the grammar school that I attended no longer have to wear uniform, nor do they have to smuggle into the school literature from outside the curriculum. The teaching staff is more heterogeneous: married or not, childless or not, Oxbridge or not. Above all, the school is no longer a grammar school. Yet even so, the rigidity of the English class system has maintained the homogeneity of the intake into the school, and the relative excellence of its examination results. What is now officially a 'neighbourhood comprehensive' is in fact a middle-class school open to middle-class children whose parents can afford to buy into the expensive local housing market. This continuity thus suggests an interesting paradox in the minds of conservatives: they both believe – in a deeply religious and passionate sense – in the virtues of the English class system, and yet at the same time they have no belief, or trust, in the system's ability to maintain itself.

The crippling lack of faith that seems to beset English conservatives was part of the culture of class that we learned at school. The school, in its leafy suburb, with its prosperous pupils was sometimes – in the exhortations and speeches of the headmistress and her colleagues – virtually the Alamo. We seemed to stand, isolated and alone, in a hostile environment, in which the natives might at any time engulf us in a tide of split infinitives and generally dissolute behaviour in the streets. One slip from a complete dedication to the norms of expected, conventional behaviour and we might end up – as we were frequently threatened – 'working in Woolworths'. Working in Woolworths was the very worst thing that could possibly happen to us, and not doing our homework and not wearing our school hats could quite easily lead to this awful fate. The angst-ridden hero of *Portnoy's Complaint* is horror-struck when he hears that the archetypal bad boy of his childhood (the unfortunate character who came – according to Portnoy's mother – from a generally sloppy home in which pyjamas were never ironed and food was not only non-kosher but also non-existent) turns out to be a Professor at Princeton. Portnoy's whole assumptive world is shattered by this news. This dissolute youth, who spent his time doing all the things that Portnoy felt guilty for merely thinking about, turns out to have succeeded in a fiercely competitive middle-class profession, and to have succeeded in that profession at a centre of WASP culture. Portnoy has to concede that his own successful career as a lawyer in New York is eclipsed by this magisterial leap into the world of goy high culture.

Not – as we would all have been the first to point out – that we were in any sense marginal. Perish the mere thought. We knew that we were part of ancient English traditions and values. Our national sense of pride was, in the 1950s, still alive and well. We had, after all, won the war, and Britain could still claim a place of significance on the world stage. We still had – just – an Empire, and although Blue Streak was falling flat on its face in the Australian desert at the same time as we were taking our O levels this kind of disaster was not yet seen as part of a general decline. More the kind of accident that could happen to anyone. So we felt we belonged in a way that Portnoy, and immigrant communities, did not. This was our country, and our historical sense was that people like us had, from the time of Cromwell, been making it a comfortable and sensible place in which to live. The slightly enlightened middle class was, therefore, our badge of identity. But even allowing for these very real material and ideological securities we were still essentially the children of wage-earners. Like all middle-class people we would have been entirely offended had we been described as 'working-class' or anything so gross as the proletariat. Yet our security depended on our parents' (particularly our father's) ability to earn a living and to earn a living that would support the detached house and the car. To do the same we would have to pass exams and learn skills that might command considerable financial rewards. We knew, and we were told (both at home and at school), that our futures needed to be earned. Thus the phrase 'working at

Woolworths' had an immediate resonance. Privileged, white, middle-class girls that we were, we nevertheless had rudimentary economic sense enough to recognise that working at Woolworths would buy only a living of a meagre kind, and certainly a living quite unlike anything that any of us had known.

Our complacent world had, therefore, a Janus-like quality to it. On the one hand, the taken-for-granted assumption that there would always be food on the table, while on the other, the frequent reminder that 'all this' was not an inherited given, but an earned acquisition, an acquisition to be safe-guarded and valued. What this dualism was teaching us was the fragility of the social world, but in an essentially conservative sense. We were not being taught the radical lesson that 'men make their history', and that men (or these days, people) can make, unmake and re-make their social reality. On the contrary, we were being taught that what has been constructed must be valued. We were seldom invited to question what had been constructed; in a very real sense we were told that the world was there and it was our responsibility to value it. But alongside the contradiction of security/insecurity that we grew up with we were also being taught two other essential features of middle-class femininity: that we must accept the values of this world and that if we were to take part in employment (or the public world) then we must do so in class-appropriate ways. In one sense, of course, we were being encouraged in a lie. As middle-class girls it was highly unlikely that we would spend our adult lives in employment. Our mothers, in general, did not have paid jobs, and the school did not encourage the employment of married teachers. Despite this, we were encouraged to think about going to university, training for professional employment and generally being serious about passing examinations and acquiring qualifications. Such an attitude on the part of the teaching staff is nowadays sometimes interpreted as a fervent feminism, a determination to ensure that girls can gain access to higher education. That determination was undoubtedly there, but so too was the determination (and this was particularly true on the part of the parents) that middle-class girls should remain in a middle-class world. The surest way to do this was, in the 1950s and the 1960s, to go to university or training college or medical school or some other enclave of middle-class expectations and aspirations.

One incident that occurred in my school days illustrates this painful ambivalence towards education for girls. In a sixth form discussion about careers (organised and chaired by the Headmistress, since this was a Serious Subject) we were all asked, in turn, about our future plans. Most of us managed to come out with some appropriate and acceptable answer. Then one unfortunate girl replied that in her future career she hoped 'to meet people'. There was an awful silence. Then the Headmistress asked exactly what this girl meant. Without waiting for a reply, the Headmistress said in tones of icy dislike and contempt: 'I suppose you want to meet men. There is hardly any point in asking you serious questions about your future.' A hushed room waited for the next onslaught, but the moment – and the Headmistress's wrath – passed, and we turned to a discussion of the A levels most appropriate for gaining entry to a training college. But the conversation was not the same. Whatever ease there had been had vanished and we were left with the uneasy feeling that the Headmistress had denounced for all of us the mere possibility of adult sexual relations with men. It was baffling. We were laughed at in our junior years in the school if we had romantic enthusiasms for the staff or the older girls, yet condemned if we displayed an interest in boys. At the same time we all (or virtually all) came from families constructed through the most orthodox mechanisms of conventional patriarchy: marriage and female economic dependence was the norm of our backgrounds. How were we going to achieve that? Had the poor unfortunate who wanted to meet people told one of those unacceptable public truths that no one wants to hear? We strongly suspected that such was the case, that a skeleton had been well and truly let out of a cupboard. The attempt to slam the door by the Headmistress merely emphasised the lengths to which the culture was prepared to go to deny and yet tacitly maintain conventional sexuality.

Denial of the realities of adult middle-class life was thus in a real sense a part of the culture of the school. We lived in a semi-fictional world in which education, and educational success, mattered more than anything else. If we chose to believe in this fiction then we could be assured of adult success, and we could also be assured of the approval and support of the school. But like all fictional worlds – or worlds constructed through strictly controlled and regulated values and beliefs – this world had to be thoroughly policed and thoroughly systematic. Hence the dislike of influences outside the school, the taste for uniform and the condemnation of those who raised the possibility of divergence and difference in this sealed world. If we had cheerfully expressed no interest in education and its rewards for girls – and said instead that meeting a husband with a substantial income was a much more important goal – then we would have left the school, and its teachers, with little rationale for their existence. It would have been rather like expressing contempt for or opposition to colonialism while employed in a colonial army or police force: we had to go on believing in our given purpose in order to make any sense of the emphasis on discipline, on hard work and on a degree of social exclusivity. Letting in the youth culture or non-academic pursuits would have meant letting in other values and other goals.

The world of the traditional grammar school, with its social limitations and its single-minded pursuit of success in exams was a world which in Britain of the 1950s and the 1960s provided an apparently perfectly coherent and congruent training ground for the managers – and their wives – of the new Elizabethan world. We were told, repeatedly, that we lived in a 'modern' world, and that in this 'modern' world education was vitally important. At the same time as we were all citizens of a modern, and modernising, Britain we were also citizens of a country with a proud history and a glorious recent past. We had, after all, recently defeated (yet again) the Germans. The peace of the world was, we were assured, safe in the hands of a responsible government. If only the Russians did not suddenly develop a particularly aggressive foreign policy, and if only the trade unions remained content to believe that they had 'never had it so good', then there seemed to be no reason why our future should not be safe. As we entered the sixth form, and as the world entered the 1960s, it did begin to look as if a more actively interventionist stance might be necessary in the economy. Words such as 'efficiency' and 'management' began to be part of our essays on the modern world and a certain politicisation began to creep into our assumptions about the world. The middle class was, if only marginally and if only occasionally, being asked to consider its place in the world. Serious middle-class figures, from serious middle-class universities, started to make noises about the future of Britain and the need for radical reform. Some, although by no means all, of the debates that gave rise to the Robbins Report and subsequent reforming legislation of the late 1960s on moral issues began to be part of sixth form debates. Views about the role of women, the nature of the family and the role of higher education, which had had the status of certainties in the 1950s, began to look more ambiguous.

Our part in all this seemed to be at the time to receive the news of these changes and to continue taking our examinations. In retrospect, what we were being asked to do was to learn a set of new assumptions about middle-class life and labour. Hitherto, the world of the British middle class had been relatively secure and (like that of the upper class) relatively sealed. Class divisions in British society had been both material (which they have remained) and cultural. The culture that we had learned as schoolchildren had had a specific quality that made it instantly recognisable and instantly apparent. Hence the cultural and social homogeneity of my school days and hence the appeal to the conservatively-minded of the idea of the grammar school. Riddled with contradictions as the schools were – crucially over the matters of education for girls and the limits of the importance of education in, and to, the class structure – they nevertheless maintained a homogeneous world which could even absorb bright children from the working class and produce a standard grammar school child. The power of the institution, therefore, was that it could apparently be relied upon to institutionalise and do for middle-class children what the public schools so effectively did for upper-class children. A reliable product, the grammar school child, emerged at the end of a seven-year education, and the product was reliably well schooled in writing legibly, writing grammatically, being punctual and having at least the appearance of respect for authority. We knew, even if we sometimes forgot, that it was polite to stand up when people older than ourselves came into a room, that you did not hold

41

your knife like a pen and that relations with adults involved a litany of silence and gratitude. We knew, in short, how to behave ourselves in public.

Unfortunately for the middle class, particularly for its more traditional sections, the public and the public world was beginning to change. The social order – the world that would predictably evaluate us – was changing and losing that single-minded absolutism that it had once had. By the mid-1960s it had finally become apparent that quite respectable, married, middle-class women did not always wear hats and gloves, sometimes they even wore trousers and smoked cigarettes. Middle-class adolescents began to perceive that out there, on the urban streets, were working-class boys and girls who were spending time in the company of the opposite sex and who were buying and wearing clothes of a positively subversive chic. The respectable comics and magazines of our childhood and adolescence (*Girl, Eagle, The Young Elizabethan*) had been full of stories of jolly schoolchildren (generally wearing school uniform) having jolly adventures. Alongside these fictional tales were life histories of appropriate heroes and heroines. *Girl*, when I read it, specialised in the life histories of Victorian female missionaries. Consequently, I had read about Gladys Aylward long before Ingrid Bergman became the archetypal Hollywood missionary in *The Inn of the Sixth Happiness*. These tales were yet another instance of the endless paradox of bourgeois feminism: the women portrayed in the tales *were* independent, bold and courageous but they lived out those qualities within the context of entirely bourgeois values. Needless to say, *Girl* did not include the lives of Rosa Luxemburg, Alexandra Kollontai or Simone de Beauvoir in its list of great women. We were offered as examples of the 'good life' people who lived lives of often quite ruthless independence. What we were not told about was the youth culture of the 1950s; for information about that we had to turn to the banned underground literature of working-class comics and teenage magazines.

But by the end of the 1950s the mould was beginning to crack. In one of its editions in the late 1950s *The Young Elizabethan* instituted a problem page and began to publish what it described as 'fashion hints'. The first question put to the agony aunt behind the problem page was the appropriate age at which girls might a) wear high heels, b) wear make-up, and c) go out alone with a member of the opposite sex. The first significance of these questions is that anyone felt that they were worth asking. The second significance is the assumption that anyone would take any notice of the answers. Inevitably, the answers bordered on the conservative. Both high heels and make-up were banned until the age of at least sixteen and going out with a member of the opposite sex was not something that anyone could properly do until the age of seventeen or eighteen. Reading this advice at the age of thirteen I reflected that it would be a long time before the world would really begin, and that since I already possessed a pair of shoes with (very low) stiletto heels I was doomed to three years of illicit footwear. So great and so all-pervasive was my internalisation of these commandments that the shoes went completely out of fashion long before I felt I was 'officially' old enough to wear them. Along with my friends I lived a secret life of fascination with adult clothes. The great *rite de passage* in our lives, universally longed for, was the prize-giving that followed school-leaving. To this we could return wearing our own clothes and it was the occasion of the most furious competition. We were supposedly there to be congratulated on our A level results and our success at gaining university entrance. No doubt these successes pleased the Headmistress and the Board of Governors. As far as we were concerned the brilliant results counted for nothing compared to our appearance in front of our peers. The real winners in that prize-giving were not awarded the school prizes, they were those who were awarded gasps of admiration by the other pupils. The occasion was one at which the values of the school and the values of the real world became transparent: we had accepted seven years of giving education the primary importance in our lives, now we turned around and said with some defiance that here, in this bold statement of fashion and the possibilities of sexual attraction, are other values and other priorities. Among the school leavers in my year was a girl who became a model with the Lucie Clayton agency as soon as she left school. Her breathtaking appearance, the total assurance of her clothes and the absolute confidence she radiated of being perfectly dressed made us all immediately, and vividly, aware that outside the sexual segregation and the drab uniform of our adolescent years there lay a world in which success had a wider meaning than that of academic performance.

Central to the alternative model of success with which we challenged the school was our degree of success with men. Despite living in an entirely female environment for virtually all our adolescent life we were expected to know how to relate, in ways appropriate to middle-class norms and mores, to men. The sub-text of our lives while at school was therefore that of how we were going to learn to do this, and how we were going to ensure male affection. Being interested in boys was generally thought vulgar, being not interested in boys was regarded as peculiar. Being wildly in love with a boy was regarded as romantic, letting that boy know was regarded as fast. The ideal was to be adored by a male other for whom one entertained a secret passion. Women, and girls, were expected to be not just sexually passive, but also emotionally passive. It was not up to us, we learnt and were told, to express our feelings. Little wonder then that the heroines of Jane Austen were so admired: only the young and unbelievably silly heroines admitted to sexual or romantic interest. We were not told, or encouraged to recognise, that Jane Austen herself grew out of this idea and that her last novel was to include a reconciliation and a claiming between lovers as passionate and as emotionally assertive as anything in fiction. Silence reigned over the issue of the nature of sexual attraction just as surely as it reigned over other issues that suggested problems associated with anything other than a norm of conventional heterosexuality. Nice, ordinary people got married to nice, ordinary people and then led nice, ordinary lives in which their children went to grammar school.

Unfortunately for this tidy, and compartmentalised, world, people in the wider world outside the English Home Counties began to demand a share in both the prosperity and the social privilege of the English middle class. Abroad, the colonies asserted their rights to self-determination and at home the working class demanded that the prosperity of the consumer boom of the 1950s should be more equally shared. Sections of the middle class, particularly the professional class, began to recognise that in order to maintain their position in the class structure they would have to have greater guaranteed access to higher education and to the recognition by society as a whole of the importance of professional skills. For a brief period in its history, the Labour Party, in its publications and broadcasts prior to the 1964 General Election, managed to capture for itself the earnest managerialism and belief in rational, technocratic progress of sections of the middle class. Harold Wilson's speeches about the 'white heat of the technological revolution' meant little to most of us, since we had little idea what a technological revolution was, but the times were clearly moving in a new direction and what was being made fashionable, and part of the being of a modern person, was a certain kind of modernity. Accepting and using technology was part of this modernity and with it went a new emphasis on efficiency and rapidity in movement and appearance. The election of John F. Kennedy as President of the United States suggested youth as a heroic character. Here was a man in his early forties who moved with an informal, windswept ease quite unlike the stiff formality of his predecessors and quite unlike the other leaders of the major super-powers. In our innocence we did not know, and were certainly not told, that Kennedy was a far from appropriate hero for well brought up young girls and that his road to power, like that of his father, was paved with machinations and deviations very far from the bourgeois ideal.

Yet Kennedy represented to many of us the first real hero of our adult lives. In a generation that had few media stars at its disposal, the young President of the United States became the kind of leader, and the kind of man, that adolescent dreams were made of. When he was assassinated and replaced by the far more avuncular figure of Lyndon Johnson, it was a matter of almost personal grief. But the school never mentioned, publicly, the assassination. Since Kennedy was shot on what was, in England, a Friday evening there was no occasion until Monday morning for the school to comment. And the school – in the person of the Headmistress – did not. It was the first instance of the public silence that I remember. Going to school on that Monday morning I had wondered what 'they' would say. I had watched David Frost and the 'That Was the Week That Was' team produce a sober and sombre valedictory for Kennedy and every

Sunday newspaper had been dominated by news and interpretation of Dallas. Surely at Monday morning assembly we would offer up a prayer or two for the people of the United States or the family of the dead man. Nothing. We sang, we prayed and received the usual notices about games fixtures and timetable changes. Since we took many of our views on how to interpret the public world from the Headmistress we left that school assembly with the distinct impression that the assassination of a President of the United States was not something that it was appropriate to talk about. We returned to our classrooms aware that something had not been said. We did not know how to say it, or even what it was we should be saying. Silence fell on the event and our first brush with a public death left us no more educated in the ability to recognise and record death and loss.

The assassination of Kennedy demonstrated to many of us the limitations of the school at dealing with the world outside. We certainly did not recognise this incapacity at the time, it was just another of those mysteries of the adult world that we were still piecing together, but in retrospect I recognise part of a pattern of silence and evasion that Laing and others were later to argue was typical of bourgeois experience and bourgeois expectations. If Kennedy's assassination had been discussed, then it might have opened up all kinds of issues about the politics, and the political decisions, of the dead President. Moreover, grief might have been expressed and with it the kind of raw emotion that had been ruled out of order since our childhoods. The school had two other brushes with death while I was there and on both occasions the pattern was similar. The first instance was the sudden death in a car crash of an extremely popular Head Girl. We walked into assembly one morning and were told that on the previous evening Rosanne had been killed. And then the Headmistress went on with the service. There were no words of grief, no suggestion that this was any kind of different announcement from the hockey match results. The tears and sobs of her friends were drowned by the usual chorus of hymn singing, and after assembly the girls most upset by their friend's death were simply sent home. Those of us who remained spent the rest of the day in half-empty classrooms feeling that somehow we should have been more upset, and yet somehow it was not quite right to be very upset. Again, a spontaneous emotional reaction had been tidied away and defined as distinct from the concerns of the institution.

This English (or perhaps, Anglo-Saxon) reaction to grief was to become – like the bourgeois silence – a focus for critiques of British institutional practice in the late 1960s. Hospitals inevitably bore the brunt of the criticism. Too many people had had their grief at death and bereavement tidied up by hospital practice for studies and personal accounts that described the trauma of the sudden separation from the dead not to strike a familiar note. Decent people were supposed to leave the corpse and not make exhibitions of themselves by clinging to the departed. Hence part of the problem in Kennedy's death. He had not died a seemly, private death but had been shot in front of millions. Worse, perhaps, was that his widow had reacted by the public expression of the realisation of imminent loss. Jacqueline Kennedy did not bother to change her clothes after the assassination, nor did she bother to disguise the desperation of her anguish. The language and form most commonly used for writing essays about the more conventional aspects of Shakespeare and Keats was not quite up to describing, or integrating into its understanding of human experience, events such as these.

Both these quite unconnected deaths – Kennedy and our sixth form contemporary – elicited no discussion from the school other than the remark that both were 'tragedies'. The other death that occurred, at about the same time, was far more ambiguous. A fellow sixth former killed herself after some months of miserable depression. In retrospect, the family situation of this girl was sufficient to create profound depression and misery in anyone. An overbearing, authoritarian father (but a distinguished local citizen in that he was the Headmaster of a local boys' secondary modern school), a meek mother and a cast completed by a runaway, openly defiant older brother and an adored, pampered younger sister. The middle child, gawky, over-tall and fiercely loyal to her mother, gradually became more and more silent as the weight of the father's disapproval became heavier and heavier. To the school, the silence, the withdrawal, were inexplicable. Suddenly, one of their bright sixth form pupils simply stopped performing. We wrote her homework and finished her essays but could not understand the degree, or the depths, of her refusal. One day she simply did not go home, the police visited her classmates and she was pronounced missing. The next day she was found dead. Reconciling her strong sense of loyalty and duty to her parents with her equally strong sense of dislike of their various inadequacies, she had found the contradiction of these two emotions impossible to live with. As a 'good girl' she had blamed herself and chosen the indirect anger of suicide. Inevitably, the school did not announce this death. The Sixth Form was assembled and warned that they must not discuss the death, either with each other or with people outside the school. The fact that nobody outside the school wanted to discuss the death meant nothing. The subject was pronounced closed, even though we knew that many of our parents rapidly took sides on the matter. The mould of middle-class convention that we had assumed to be unshakeable revealed its internal differences. The liberal parents blamed the father, the more authoritarian parents either blamed the girl or voiced the opinion that there must have been 'something wrong with her'.

This glimpse into other people's families, and the human results of other people's family lives, thus suggested to us a world that was more complicated than the school chose to assume. At school, good, caring families were taken as the norm. If a note was sent to our parents, it was assumed that a) our parents were both there to read it, and that b) our parents would act in our best interests. Equally, it was expected that since we were cared for, we would 'honour our fathers and mothers'. This was our given model of reciprocity, and all parents were supposed to conform to it. But adolescent girls who committed suicide gave the lie – albeit in the most extreme form – to this surface normality and the assumption of a common way of life and a common set of expectations. Behind those middle-class façades, and those ranks of middle-class uniforms, there lay difference, and difference of a kind that was – on some issues – irreconcilable. When I heard my father and the father of my closest friend concurring in the view that the father of the girl who committed suicide ought not to have anything to do with children (let alone his own) then I realised that even if we all looked the same, talked the same and on the whole voted the same way, there were differences in our world that we were not told about. Grammar schools made much of the common ground – for the middle class they provided a shared experience and a shared set of manners and coded social behaviour. But difference was there and rapidly exposed by difficult or traumatic episodes. Maintaining social cohesion could be achieved, but it was achieved at the cost of denying difference and refusing many of the contradictions and complexities of adult experience. Central to this pattern of denial was the school's relation with the issue of gender. What follows in the next chapter is, therefore, a collective case history of the loss of the female body.

3

Body Language

Part of the initiation ceremony of going to grammar school was examination by a doctor, in the presence of the school's Headmistress and our mothers. The examination largely consisted of seeing if we stood up straight (otherwise we were put down for remedial exercises in the school's Remedial Room), could stand on our toes and perform other tests of minimal physical competence. But at the end of the examination, which also involved the cross-questioning of our mothers about our behaviour as if we were not there, the school doctor took a rapid peep into our knickers. It was so sudden that it constituted a particularly intrusive kind of invasion. It also formed the immediate topic of conversation among the new girls on their first day at school. A bold spirit expressed the view that she hoped that the dreadful doctor would not be seen again and that 'she' had done the most awful thing. This recollection thus provoked a chorus of similarly outraged eleven year olds. Our sense of privacy may not have mattered to adults, or to adult doctors, but it certainly mattered to us and we were to a person deeply offended by this perfunctory and unexpected examination. The incident established the tenor of our relationship with the school and with the school and our bodies that was to last until we left.

The central assumption of the medical examination as we saw it was that the school, and adults who had any association with the body at the school, was dismissive of the body as anything but a body. 'Nobody will be looking at you' and 'you are all the same' were remarks that we heard over and over again. We knew that both remarks were utterly and entirely untrue, and indeed were contradicted by many of the other practices of the school. If nobody was looking at us, and if we were all the same, why was it that there was such a prohibition on sunbathing near the public paths in summer and why did some girls attract so much more obvious public attention than others? We knew, and we strongly suspected that they knew, that being physically attractive mattered. Indeed, physical attraction and appeal did not just matter, it was going to be central to our experiences and our very circumstances after we left school.

But thinking about how we looked was part of the hidden and underground culture of the school. From the moment that we entered the school at the age of eleven to the moment when we left at the age of eighteen we were deeply conscious not just of how we looked but of how other people looked. We assessed each other critically, and often far from sympathetically, and calculated our various chances of being attractive, very attractive or stunningly and irresistibly attractive. Our role models, our heroines changed as the years changed but a fairly consistent pattern remained: the favoured look-alike was tall (but not so tall as to make men feel interior), slim (and teenage girls and fat constituted a major preoccupation as much then as now), white (we never thought any other possibility existed), with regular features and absolutely no distinguishing irregularities. Audrey Hepburn was much in vogue; Doris Day and her fellow American actresses had only a limited following. When I first entered the school Petula Clark was regarded as an appropriate model. By the time I left (in 1964) the new moral and social pluralism was such that the model woman included Jacqueline Kennedy, Juliette Greco, Brigitte Bardot and again (and still) Petula Clark. A year later the list had extended to include Julie Christie, Vanessa Redgrave and Mia Farrow. Choosing a model was far from random: identify with a figure such as Cilla Black and you risked the accusation of 'tarty', just as identification with Sophia Loren or Gina Lollobrigida suggested that you were really not-quite-nice. By 1964 I had discovered the world of Hollywood in the 1930s; that opened up the possibility of those figures of super-cool female poise such as Greta Garbo,

Katharine Hepburn, Bette Davis and Joan Crawford. These women were not only mistresses of their own fate, they were also (or appeared on screen) tall.

This preoccupation with finding a female role model who was over 5'6" tall reflected one of the two central obsessions of our teenage years as far as the body was concerned. One was height, the other was weight. About height we could do little except pray that we would not grow too tall. If we did, by some awful and fiendish accident, grow and grow, then we also adopted dreadful slouches and postures in which one permanently sagged. Both strategies were designed to minimise our awful inches and reduce us to the kind of height that made it possible for boys to choose us as dancing partners. This obsession with being smaller than boys was obviously universal among girls in the West in the 1950s. Sylvia Plath wrote sharply to her mother in the late 1950s, reprimanding her for suggesting that her baby daughter should be given drugs to stem her growth. Plath wrote that she had had no difficulty in finding 'a wonderfully tall husband' and there was every possibility that her daughter would be equally fortunate. Two points are significant about this exchange. The first is that Plath had, prior to her meeting and marriage with Ted Hughes, been much dismayed by her height. Boyfriends were assessed in terms of *their* height, and one of the men whom Plath most admired and liked was written off as a serious marriage partner because he was short. Conversely, a young man for whom Sylvia Plath did not have much liking was tolerated and encouraged because physically he allowed Sylvia to conform to the western expectation of the woman being shorter than her male partner. So if Sylvia was annoyed with her mother – and the tone certainly suggests a degree of irritation – then the irritation may well have arisen out of a recognition that she, Sylvia, shared the same view as her mother – namely, that women should not be too tall.

The second feature of this exchange is that Mrs Plath is asserting, quite unselfconsciously, a physical expectation, and a physical stereotype, as a moral norm. Being not too tall is 'good' for women, in the same way as being tidy or clean or good at arithmetic is an excellent and valuable attribute. The moral appearance of the body, or the morality of appearance, was thus articulated forcefully by Mrs Plath, and probably by millions of other mothers and their daughters. Very few women, in fact, do grow to be exceptionally tall (in the same way as most men do not) but it was nevertheless an awful spectre of adolesence, and a spectre reinforced by the professional expectations of certain archetypically feminine occupations. Of the occupations which I remember as having height qualfications, those of being a ballet dancer or an air hostess were the two most commonly cited examples. Few of us aspired to either of these occupations but they somehow had a mythical status as examples of things that we could not do if we grew too tall. If we grew too tall we would thus never make the *corps de ballet*; anyone over 5'3" would make the dance of the four little cygnets look superbly ridiculous and an air hostess over 5'5" would presumably be in constant risk of concussion from the ceiling of the aeroplane. If we longed to dance professionally, we could always be dancers in the world of entertainment. Vulgar, grinning chorus girls were quite ofen very tall. But to enter the sacred world of classical ballet the norm was the anorexic sylph of 5'3". To a large extent this norm has persisted and although norms in dance and ballet have changed to a certain extent one of the ideals of female perfection is still the tiny, slight ballet dancer.

To be slight, and certainly not too tall, was thus one fervent wish in our adolescent hearts. The second wish – and one which persists with real vigour to this day – was the determination not to be fat. Here morality took a truly firm hand. Being tall could always be explained by an unlucky chance of nature (most particularly, having a tall father). But being fat was all your own fault. Nobody but yourself was to blame if you were either a bit overweight, rather podgy or just downright enormous. In those innocent days few of our parents or teachers knew about anorexia nervosa and other eating disorders. If we professed concern about our weight then we were told that a) we were being silly and that b) we ate too much rubbish. Back in the 1950s it was difficult not to eat a diet that was full of sugar and fat. Those pre-Yudkin days did not contain the same degree of self-consciousness about what people ate. Indeed, in an era in which rationing had only just ended, and in which mass famine had been a phenomenon not just of the Third World but of

Western Europe, refusing food for whatever reasons smacked of the most awful ingratitude and selfishness. We were not (quite) told to eat up our suet pudding because millions of people would be glad of it, but we were told (almost every lunch-time) that being fussy about food and wasting it were very close to sin. So we were encouraged to eat, and encouraged to eat whatever was offered. At the same time we were not expected to worry about the end-result of eating a high fat and carbohydrate diet. Eating was in, dieting was out.

Nevertheless, in a surreptitious and determined way most of the school over the age of fourteen practised, more or less consistently, some form of diet and some form of fairly rigorous policing of weight and fat. Fat girls were mocked and they were laughed at. Moreover, in a school in which games and gymnastics were compulsory, there was no way of disguising personal appearance. Every games class, every gymnastics class must have been torture for the fat or the podgy. The gymnastics class was graded according to ability. The distinctions in ability corresponded absolutely with conformity to the western ideal of woman: those slim girls of average height were part of division one, the fat, indolent and short-sighted were part of division two, if not division three. There was no conception in those days of fat being beautiful, let alone a feminist issue, or indeed anything other than fat being gross and a sign of serious self-indulgence and moral failing. Conformity to rigid stereotypes of the female body was thus reinforced and institutionalised at least once a day in the compulsory periods of physical activity. The agonies of adolescence are no doubt part of the experience of every child in western culture, even if distinct for girls and boys. Our agonies centred on our weight and our height, with matters such as acne and squint coming a close second.

Our interest, intense and obsessive, in how we looked, was, of course, in contradiction to the ethos and the practices of the school. We wore compulsory uniform throughout our seven years at grammar school, and the wearing of uniform was publicly and frequently defended and rationalised on the grounds that this compulsory and universal regimentation in navy blue serge would keep our minds off our appearance and our bodies. The passage in *Jane Eyre* in which Mr Brocklehurst orders the hair of a schoolgirl to be cut on the grounds that the hair is too curly and too frivolous struck a chord in our collective understanding. We were not actually threatened with having our hair cut off, but our appearance was policed with much the same kind of enthusiasm as had been the case in the days of Jane Eyre. The contradiction, and the paradox, of this constant vigilance and policing (the endless watching for the non-regulation hair slide or the frilly petticoat) was that our appearance was not supposed to matter. The whole function of school uniform we were repeatedly told was that we could come to school and think only of our school work. In the carefully managed and arranged debates on whether or not we should wear school uniform the 'right' side always brought to our attention the miserable lives that we would lead if we had to consider what to wear when we got out of bed in the morning. Held up to us as an example of the horrible possibilities of not wearing uniform was the sad case of our sisters at non-selective schools (that is, at secondary moderns) who were confronted every morning by the terrible anguish of not knowing what to wear. Imagine, we were told, what it must be like to get out of bed and face the overwhelming existential agony of deciding between a blue or green sweater and a straight or pleated skirt. How we longed to share this anguish, and how we knew that whatever we were told, wearing a uniform did *not* eliminate thinking about what to wear. What we thought about was how to wear our uniform and what we looked like in it. Repression could go so far, but it could not suppress the fertile imaginations of schoolgirls about their appearance.

Growing older, and larger, in this culture which both denied and emphasised the importance of appearance, we absorbed the information that part of our social and moral definition was our appearance. The norm of a conventional British woman for our teachers was probably an amalgam of Celia Johnson and the Queen. Both were clearly ladies, and if Celia Johnson did teeter on the brink of adultery then at least the physical squalor of the surroundings in which the awful act might occur did deter her from entirely unlady-like behaviour. We were expected to know how far to go and to recognise (like Celia Johnson in *Brief*

Encounter) the physical surroundings that indicated squalor and immorality. We were certainly not told about adultery in any sense, either literal or metaphorical, but we were taught to recognise the physical signs of moral failing. Being fat, being dirty, being generally slovenly were all part of the immoral person. The curious aspect of these signs and signals was that they were so close to some perfectly acceptable, indeed charming, attributes. Thus being a bit untidy, a bit grubby or even just slightly less than immaculate were all signs of a healthy attitude to clothes and the body. Being too immaculate and too tidy was somehow not quite nice, in the same way as being interested in one's appearance was definitely not nice.

What was being denied, suppressed and condemned in this pattern of the regulation of appearance was our narcissism. The dangers of self-absorption and self-interest were spelt out to us, alongside the veneration of psychic health in the pursuit of community and communal aims. Here, we faced a fundamental contradiction of bourgeois life. We were told to subordinate our individual interests and tastes to those of the community: choosing our own clothes, we were told in those arranged 'debates', might make us look like an untidy group, rather than a neat troop. Standing in front of the mirror in the school cloakroom for too long meant that first, we were not performing some other, more socially useful task and second, we were blocking the mirror that other people might want to use. These 'other people' that we had to think about popped up with monotonous regularity in the instructions about the world that we received. It was wrong to shout or speak too loudly, in case 'other people' were disturbed, it was wrong to get angry or walk in too large a group or make jokes in public in case 'other people' should in some way be offended. The others we had to think about sat on our shoulders like Long John Silver's parrot: always there, always ready with a repetitive reminder of what to do and how to behave. But the contradiction in this, and the contradiction that we were learning about our class and its culture, was that we had to compete against each other and make sure that our interests triumphed over those of the person next to us. We could not all get distinctions in our examinations, or scholarships to universities, or even university places. Since the major motive of our school was encouraging and teaching us to do all these things we were faced, each and every day, by a complex and contradictory lesson in how to behave. On the one hand, we were rewarded for being polite, helpful, tidy and good at being part of a group. On the other, we were rewarded a great deal more for being particulary good at examinations. Academic success, we quickly realised, could cancel out a lot of failings in terms of personal behaviour and what was generally, if vaguely, referred to as our 'attitude'.

Because we knew that our academic abilities mattered to the school we quickly came to realise that although the school constituted one of the 'others' in our social and moral universe there were further significant others in the world. The first of these was the world of higher education, and that was a world which had a central importance for many of us, and all of our teachers. But the second other who dominated our thinking was the male sex. Thus we lived in a world of moral and social pluralism: there was not a single standard of aspirations but a varied one. We had to meet, and conform to, the school's expectations about us, and many of these expectations were vague as well as confused. At the same time we aspired to success in two areas that were – and to a certain extent still are – mutually contradictory. The worlds were those of sex and learning. We wanted to succeed academically and yet at the same time we wanted, desperately, to succeed with boys.

Volumes have been written about what Mirra Komarovsky described almost forty years ago, as 'cultural contradictions and sex roles'.[4] In an article about female college students in the United States in the late 1940s Mirra Komarovsky pointed out that bright, academically gifted women often denied their abilities and talents in order to avoid alienating men. Men, the students assumed, would be put off by bright women. Thus the students hid their intellectual competence and adopted devious and circuitous ploys in order to suggest that any academic success that they did have was a matter of chance or luck. The label 'blue-stocking' held, for these girls, a fearsome suggestion of spinsterhood, failure at heterosexuality and lack of sexual appeal to men. The article, if the first in western sociology to notice and define this phenomenon, was hardly original in that throughout the eighteenth and nineteenth centuries a long tradition of women (and occasionally men) writers had noticed the fear of women at appearing 'clever' or 'brainy'. 'Silliness' in women had been attacked by Jane Austen, Charlotte Brontë, George Eliot and virtually every major woman writer long before sociology was an established discipline. Yet what Komarovsky did (and in the same vein what Betty Friedan and Germaine Greer were to do in later works in the 1960s and 1970s) was to identify within a culture the complexities of expectations about the behaviour of women and the values of men.

We lived within this contradiction and we lived, in the school, among women who had been forced to make an either/or choice between marriage and a career. It was only in 1948 that the British Home Civil Service had abolished the marriage disqualification for women, and up to this time many grammar schools had followed the example of the Civil Service and barred married women from employment. Although the ban was not universal, and did vary from area to area, the general British assumption was that marriage, for women, did not combine with a career in teaching, particularly in secondary teaching. Occasionally, some local authorities did allow married women to stay in post, but this was certainly a far from general pattern and what was quite unknown was married women with young children having posts in teaching. When the young, married staff of my school became pregnant they rapidly left and as far as I recall were never seen again. They disappeared into a shadowy world of home and children and we were left with the distinct impression that they had contracted some rather dreadful disease and been sent off to a distant sanatorium to recover. Having children, being married and becoming part of the universal Janet and John world that we all emerged from was thus a quite distinct experience as far as the majority of our teachers was concerned. The valiant spinsters who taught us lived in small flats or shared houses with other women. They biked to school, wore flat, sensible shoes and white ankle socks and appeared, even at the age of forty or fifty, to be still living out their own student days. Our teachers talked with nostalgia of their years at Oxford, Cambridge and Bedford College and were firmly moulded in their habits and tastes by the cloistered, semi-feminist worlds from which they emerged. Equally, many of us – going up to university in the heady days of the 1960s and early 1970s – found it difficult later to shake off the language of student protest and disaffection. Institutionalisation by and through education thus was and remains a feature of English life. Our teachers were marked by their universities, we were marked by our school and in turn by our universities.

But in many ways our experiences at university were to differ radically from those of the people who taught us. We mocked and scorned our teachers' lack of interest in dress and appearance and longed for the day when we could shake off our navy blue serge for real, grown-up clothes. Going to university (or training college) was for us an opportunity which we pictured partly in terms of educational interest and yet rather more in terms of the social opportunities we fondly imagined would be there, as well as the endless possibilities for dressing in our clothes. For us, leaving school and going out into the world was not a matter of emancipation from the world of men and male control, but entry into a world populated by thousands and thousands of male others. Here, in a generation, was a major shift in the history of women's education (and the attitude of women to education). The women who taught us had gone up to university in the late 1920s and early 1930s. They had been contemporaries of Barbara Pym, Dorothy L. Sayers and countless other, less famous women at the Oxbridge women's colleges. Like these women, they had been taught by women and taught that the education they were receiving was a privilege and, above all, a matter of great seriousness. In Barbara Pym's diaries she recalls that she frequently felt guilty about her own frivolous occupations and interests; thinking about what to wear for a tutorial was not, she knew very well, at all the correct attitude to education. This view of education was, of course, inevitable in that many of the women teaching at Oxbridge between the wars had had to fight, and fight again, in order to gain entry to these august patriarchal institutions. Once there, it must have become rapidly apparent that although excellent, serious work was done by some students and staff there was also a great deal of social education at Oxbridge that had everything to do with male public school friendship networks and very little to do with that apparent seriousness of purpose that the universities had always paid lip-service to.

But having fought their way in, and having only a precarious hold on the real institutional power (not to mention material resources) of the major universities, women continued to play by the formal rules. Thus what they passed on to their students, and what their students passed on to us, was a view of education which regarded education as a moral crusade, a process of such value that its existence and its inherent value were above and beyond questioning. This attitude was the dominant attitude of the school, in so far as the school was represented by official staff publications and endorsements. However, this attitude was very far from the attitude of the majority of the students. We valued, in various degrees, our studies and many of us enjoyed them. What we did not subscribe to was the view that being educated, going to university, constituted the good life. In our simple and frivolous adolescent minds we associated education for women with ankle socks and bicycles. Our own aspirations ran in the direction of cars, men and fashionable clothes. If education was a means to this (and given the sex ratio of students in higher education in Britain in the early 1960s the chances of meeting men in universities were very considerable) then education certainly had an important part to play in our view of our futures. If, on the other hand, education was not to be about any of these things, then the interest of education was much diminished. We longed to enter what we saw as the glamorous adult world, an adult world which was peopled by men.

Our enthusiasm, then, was for an entry into the patriarchal world. The very women who had battled for entry into this world had made themselves unacceptable to us as role models because they seemed to have rejected men. This very curious paradox was a major element in our thinking in the sixth form about where to go to university and what to study. Oxford and Cambridge held sway because of their social domination of British life. But women's colleges at other universities held no attraction for us; our choices were all for the large civic universities where we knew that we would be heavily outnumbered by male students. Despite the enthusiasm of our teachers for such 'polite' universities as Exeter and Bristol we nevertheless entertained enthusiasms for Birmingham, Manchester and the mixed colleges of London University. Entry to any university in those days was highly selective (we were asked for grades at A level that would now make many an Admissions Officer of a university faint with enthusiasm) and so we devoted much care to our selection.

Once there, our careers were varied. Of the year that went up to university in 1964 several friends and acquaintances were actually sent down from university for failing first year examinations. In one case, a friend of mine – reading Fine Arts at a distinguished provincial university – was sent down *without appeal* for failing a first year examination in Latin. In 1965 this provoked not a glimmer of outrage. Ten years later it would have probably provoked – at the very least – a student sit-in and a review by a university committee. As it was, my friend slunk home in disgrace, even though several years later she was to profit from the liberalisation of universities and return (elsewhere) to take an excellent degree. But these were the kind of controls which we took for granted. We accepted that Chaucer was an inevitable part of English Literature, that our teacher's assessment of our work was final and that the standards we had been brought up in were absolute. Our acceptance made us willing pupils, for we knew of no other standards. In the prosperous, provincial world in which we lived uniformity and conventionality were never questioned.

The impact of this world was such as to make us deeply porous to two different sets of values. Just because we were well-behaved, conventional, middle-class girls we accepted the demands of the school and we did, on the whole, obey the rules and regulations. Equally, again because we were well-behaved, conventional, middle-class girls we accepted the values of the world outside the school in which material and sexual success mattered. We became suspicious of our friendships with other girls because – by the age of fifteen or sixteen – we had learnt the norms of what Adrienne Rich was to describe in 1980 as 'compulsory heterosexuality'. We learnt that we could not live by education alone and that if we wished to buy all the goods that the new consumer society had to offer then we would have to make both material decisions and materially informed choices. Rejecting men and rejecting heterosexuality made no sense of either the social or the material lives that the majority of us wished to lead.

And so, as we worked assiduously at our examinations and expressed a reasonable amount of fervour and enthusiasm for the communal life of the school, we also developed and attempted to work out a sexual and social morality and strategy for this wider world. In this endeavour, we were given scant specific guidance by the school; on the other hand, we were given endless non-specific guidance. We thus went through seven years at school acquiring an attitude to sex and sexual morality but virtually no information about procreation, reproduction or what Kinsey described as 'human sexual relations'. Back in the 1950s and early 1960s very few schools gave lessons in what has become known as 'sex education' and we learnt our minimal lessons about reproduction in mammals from a somewhat garbled account of the activities of the rabbit. In our bright orange biology notebooks we drew pictures of male and female rabbits and learnt that from difference the next generation of rabbits emerged. Quite how, let alone why, was a mystery to all of us. The male rabbit did, at some point, 'deposit' his sperm in the female rabbit but why the female should have been used as a kind of sexual lost property office remained an unanswered, and unasked, question. We simply had no idea how these processes occurred in human beings. What was more, we had a curious, yet highly developed, resistance to knowing any more about human biology. In one of the fifth form classes on biology one of the pupils, regarded as slightly racy and a bit too interested in boys, told an almost risqué joke about a honeymoon couple. She was generally cold-shouldered and told, by one of the popular form personalities, that the joke was 'disgusting'. We all acted like characters in an Angela Brazil novel: deeply fascinated and obsessed by the idea of sex as we were, we nevertheless regarded the direct expression of this interest as quite unacceptable and socially out-of-bounds. What we had absorbed was an attitude which stated that nice girls were heterosexual and yet totally uninterested in men and sex.

Our ignorance about the mechanics of adult sexuality not-withstanding, we devoted a great deal of attention to the study of men. Our fantasy men conformed more or less exactly to the heroes of Mills and Boon and Barbara Cartland. Men were to be taller than us, with nice clean (and well-paid) professional jobs and jolly good ideas about respecting women and the values of monogamy. Love and marriage in the 1950s went together in the middle-class mind, and the public expression of sexuality was, at least to us, limited. The moral debates of the 1950s were – as Elizabeth Wilson and others have argued – about such vexed questions as 'sex before marriage' and the proper place of women.[5] A cautiously hedonistic attitude to sex was beginning to appear in the culture: sex was supposed to be enjoyable for both parties and modern couples were supposed to be able to discuss sexual matters openly and frankly. Yet as we were growing up we were not expected to mention menstruation even to our female teachers and discussions about sex and sexual morality never formed part of the curriculum. So great was the modesty of the school that the prohibition of the explicit mention of menstruation made it possible to escape physical education and swimming for weeks at a time. Since in those days it was regarded as perfectly acceptable not to play sport during a period (and to swim during a period was thought positively disgusting) we had only to mutter that we did not feel 'well' to be allowed to go and read a book or take a quiet walk. Many of us spent happy hours enjoying this happy semi-invalidism, gazing with pity at our more honest sisters.

Cultural lag takes many different forms in different societies and in the English provinces in the 1950s one of the forms that it took was the persistence of the notion of menstruation as pollution and disability. Virginia Woolf, after all, had spent a few days every month lying on a sofa for what she euphemistically described as 'the usual reason'. We were unable to take to the sofa, but we were able to stay in warm classrooms or remain fully dressed when the alternatives were semi-naked, forced physical activity. What we learnt to use effectively was the schoolgirl equivalent of the marital headache: our teachers, presumably like some husbands, were too embarrassed to question us further about our physical problems. Indeed, given that

63

the school contained some 600 pupils and a staff of some thirty teachers (all of whom were female) the silence about the subject of menstruation was astounding. One of the occasions most likely to produce immediate giggles and nudging was the sight of the Deputy Headmistress stepping up onto the dais at the morning school assembly. If the Deputy Headmistress was to take assembly then we knew that some subject associated with the cloakrooms or the lavatories or sanitary towels was going to be mentioned. The Headmistress herself did not mention these perplexing aspects of the communal life of women.

So the Deputy Headmistress would launch into the usual purposeful rendering of 'I Vow to Thee My Country' say a rapid prayer for the state of the country and then bid us sit down while she read out the notices. But her notices were read with downcast eyes and an unusually stern expression. It must have been difficult to tell 600 adolescent girls that they had yet again been responsible for blocking the lavatories without worrying about the risk of giggling and tittering. Since this unfortunate woman had the task of organising the cleaning out of the lavatories and the discussion of the problem with the male plumbers, she must have felt some anger at the silliness of our response and at the notion of hierarchy which excluded the officers from dealing with mundane matters of basic hygiene and left the NCO to try to make the troops behave. In my seven years at the school neither of the two Headmistresses ever mentioned – at least in public – the distressing subjects of lavatories and the female body. Authority maintained a complete separation from these subjects. At the time I assumed – when old enough to do more than giggle about the subject – that the Headmistresses were particularly modest people, who could not bring themselves to discuss physical functions (however general) in public. In retrospect, I recognise a pattern which associates the disposal of bodily waste with low-status people and occupations. Ward orderlies, not surgeons, actually clean up the vomit and it is a conventional practice in the West for fathers to hand their small children to the mother should the child need to have its nappy changed. In mixed secondary schools it is a common occurrence that the Headteacher is a man, the Deputy Headteacher a woman. This frequent pattern is then explained in terms of the necessity of having a Deputy Headteacher who is a woman, 'for the girls'. This telling phrase is, of course, a polite euphemism for 'someone-who-can-talk-about-periods-without-crossing-those-lines-of-social-discussion-which-organise-the-way-in-which-the-sexes-talk-about-sex-or-the-body'. It is much quicker to explain the pattern in terms of the phrase 'for the girls'.

Growing up in this institutional environment in which silence about the implications of the body was accompanied by a certain contempt for its comfort and appearance, we learned to regard school as a place of segregated activity. We took to school our heads. Many of us were happy to do this. We would have been even happier if we could have had the opportunity to leave our bodies at home. School was not comfortable and even by the standards of England in the 1950s (an age in which many middle-class homes still did not have central heating and in which efficient washing machines were still part of the domestic technology to come) the school was uncomfortable. It was uncomfortable in the sense that although the building was relatively modern (it had been purpose-built in the 1930s) it was still cold in the winter (that is from October to May) and insufficiently provided with hot water and private space. After gymnastics or games lessons we could not take showers (since there were none) and if we were dirty or sweaty then that was how we stayed for the rest of the day. If we wanted to read a book or simply have a conversation then there was nowhere to go. Nor were the staff more privileged. The thirty staff shared a single staff room in which there were five or six easy chairs. No one except the Headmistress had access to a telephone, or tea or coffee on demand. Even though we suffered less from lack of privacy than pupils at boarding schools, we still pictured life-after-school as a world in which we would have our own space and our own open access to ordinary conveniences such as hot drinks and adequate storage space for our possessions. Our comments about school often reflected this sense of lack of space; we spoke of 'getting away from this place' and 'this dump'. The school was far from a dump, but after seven years in it we had acquired a sense of a place in which nothing comfortable or attractive or convenient was allowed. We emerged well suited to living in sparse comfort in Oxbridge rooms or in Youth Hostels. Equally, we emerged largely committed to living, and working, in comfortable places.

Our sense of discomfort at school was thus in part created by the daily discomfort that our bodies suffered – the cold, the hard chairs and the dirt. But we were far from being twentieth-century Jane Eyres. We arrived at school from comfortable homes and it was only between the hours of 9 a.m. and 3.45 p.m. that we had to live in an environment that was becoming increasingly foreign to the British middle class. Our homes were gradually acquiring central heating (indeed this was a great mark of status among us), fitted carpets, properly functioning hot water systems and all the other commodities that were to be taken for granted some twenty years later. When I was at school I, like many of my contemporaries, had chilblains on my feet every winter. My two school shirts had to be hung over the fire to dry. Our relatively prosperous middle-class homes did not, in those days, have warm bedrooms or tumble driers. Our mothers frequently complained about washing machines that flooded, and many of our fathers still started their cars with starting handles. Getting a car to start in the depths of the English winter was, anyway, a risky business since there was always a reasonable chance that the water in the radiator was frozen.

When I entered grammar school in 1957 the memory of the war years, of power cuts and no domestic machinery at all was still the dominant experience. We were told not to be cold. The command was as simple as that: the statement of being cold was frequently met by the retort, 'Of course you're not'. But by the time I left grammar school in 1964 a new attitude to, and experience of, domestic comfort had emerged. Our homes had acquired domestic machinery and we had come to measure our experience by its conformity to films and advertisements that offered a comfortable, clean and physically effortless life. Indeed, our collective impression of the past (particularly the Victorian past) was that it was incredibly uncomfortable. In part, this impression was gained from the classics of English literature, which formed part of our compulsory curriculum. Oliver Twist was always short of food, Jane Eyre was often both cold and hungry, life at Wuthering Heights was positively grim and many of the characters in Thomas Hardy lived in almost animal-like squalor. The list was endless: from Mrs Gaskell we learned about the appalling conditions of the Victorian industrial cities and *Vanity Fair* contained passages of the graphic description of either aristocratic squalor or genteel poverty. Even Jane Austen was not above noticing the physical world; in an age without refrigeration she gave, in *Mansfield Park*, a vivid description of the disgusting state of sour milk. In 1955 about half the households in the United Kingdom did not have access to a refrigerator; those homes, like that of Fanny Price's family, no doubt still had rancid milk at the same time as we were collectively assuming that such things were a feature of the past.

So our sense of modernity, of belonging to a post-war, contemporary world, was in part created by our experience of the rapidly improving material and domestic conditions of the British middle class. It was no longer acceptable to be cold and dirty at home and we lived in an age of fervent home improvement and increasing personal comfort. By the time I left school I did not expect to be cold in winter or not have access to constant hot water. Our bodies had therefore acquired a set of modern expectations about the nature of comfort. We had also, and this must constitute part of the negative picture of the consumer revolution in the home, come to regard as modern and in some sense progressive, convenience foods and a daily assault on our bodies by various toiletries. By 1964 there was a great deal to buy for the body and its physical presence and presentation had become a matter not just of concern but of consumption. We became preoccupied with deodorants and sprays for the body. We noticed if our teachers wore the same blouse for two days in succession and we made life an endless misery for those of our teachers whom we suspected of never washing their hair. Tending the body to the standards of the late twentieth century had become our norm; it was apparent that some of the staff still lived in an era of weekly baths and clean clothes on Sunday. These personal details never escaped our eagle, adolescent eyes and the failure of the physical appearance of the staff to conform to our expectations and standards constituted another of the forms of difference between us. What was happening here was that we were becoming absorbed into a world of classless, or relatively classless, mass consumption in which everyone (or nearly everyone) washed and changed their clothes every day. For women of the middle class that genteel dowdiness and lack of interest in clothes that has long been the trademark of the real English 'lady' was becoming an anachronism of the past – particularly to the young. The tweed skirts and linen blouses of our teachers may have come in the first place from Aquascutum and Jaeger, but as the first place was some ten years ago we simply thought that the clothes were slightly comic. When we were told that this or that garment still 'had a lot of wear in it' we laughed. We had no interest in the functional aspect of clothes. Since all clothes, by definition, covered the body, our view was that the more fashionable the better.

The wearing of uniform for those seven long adolescent years bred in all of us, to various degrees, an intense self-consciousness about how we looked. Adolescents of both sexes are anyway preoccupied with their physical appearance; being forced to wear uniform made us not less aware of clothes and the body but more aware of both. As soon as we arrived home we changed out of the despised uniform; weekends and evenings were golden days of golden opportunities to wear our own clothes. The denial of difference produced the opposite effect – an interest in the development of difference through dress and personal adornment. The staff did not, on the whole, think that the education of girls mixed at all well with the toleration of adolescent narcissism. Thus all interest in one's personal appearance was a proscribed activity. Lingering in front of one of the two mirrors provided in a school of 600 girls was positively discouraged and we were banned from bringing small, handbag-sized mirrors to school on the totally specious grounds that a broken mirror could cause accidents. The rule was extensively broken. Every morning 600 girls trotted up the drive of the school and in the majority of the 600 satchels was a small mirror. We managed to survive with no fatal accidents from broken glass, but I doubt if we could have survived without some way of checking our personal appearance at frequent intervals. Our sense of vanity was never thwarted by the taunts of the staff that no one looked at us and that no one was interested in what we looked like. We knew better. We knew that even if in the classroom and on the hockey field we were not observed by critical eyes, there was always the walk before and after school to the bus and train station. As we grew older we also knew that even if no one looked at us twice in our school uniform it took only a rapid change of clothes to make us into people of at least passable physical interest.

We thus regarded with a measure of disbelief and contempt both the personal appearance and the advice about personal appearance given to us by the staff. We mocked the short socks, the hair bands on women in their fifties and the endless parade of pleated tweed skirts. We had to accept the institutional and the academic authority of our teachers but we did not respect them as individuals or regard them as what social scientists term 'role models'. Indeed, we wanted to be as unlike them as possible and our adolescent allegiances could have been bought by anyone in a tight skirt with a beehive hair-style. It was an attitude to a generation of brave and determined women teachers that was not, however, confined to one grammar school in south-east England. When Sylvia Plath arrived at Cambridge University on a Fulbright Scholarship in 1955 she wrote home to her mother about the women teaching her:

> I see in Cambridge, particularly among the women dons, a series of such grotesques! It is almost like a caricature series from Dickens to see our head table at Newnham. Daily we rather merciless and merry Americans, South Africans and Scottish students remark the types at the don's table, which range from a tall, cadaverous woman with purple hair (really!) to a midget Charles Addams fat creature who has to stand on a stool to get into the soup tureen. They are all very learned or brilliant (quite a different thing) in their specialised ways, but I feel that all their experience is secondary and this to me is tantamount to a kind of living death.[6]

These comments were far from exceptional in Plath's letters, and her view of teachers, particularly spinster teachers, was to appear in another, and much more critical form, in *The Bell Jar*. When Sylvia Plath met the perfect male other in the shape of Ted Hughes one of her revealing comments (again in a letter home) was that she could wear high heels when going out with Hughes.

As she wrote, 'what a blessing to wear heels with Ted and still be "little".'

So powerful was the ideology of femininity, and the shape and size appropriate for women, that a woman as highly educated and talented as Sylvia Plath should aspire to be 'little'. A great deal of ink has now been spilt on the nature of the Hughes/Plath marriage; what is significant about the relationship here is the extent to which, at least on the side of Sylvia Plath, ideologies of feminine inferiority and masculine power shaped the choices, the decisions and the behaviour of this individual. It is not that Sylvia Plath is the only woman who has ever been misled by romance, it is that education, worldly experience and a measure of affluence are no armour against some of the most trite and vulgar ideas about behaviour appropriate for men and women. And so it was, in a less intense and in a far less well-documented case in girls' grammar schools. Even if we did not seriously expect the Ted Hughes/Mr Rochester/Heathcliff figure to spring out from behind the privet hedges of our suburban homes, then we did put a premium on the appearance, at some early stage in our adult lives, of the male other who would complete and finalise our social existence. Our sense of the lives of our teachers was that their identities were seriously lacking. Even if they appeared perfectly happy and healthy (which they certainly did) they still did not measure up to our picture of the socially 'whole' person. Their academic strengths, their range of interests, their ability to cope very patiently (and year after year) with their often silly and recalcitrant pupils, all these qualities counted for nothing against their serious deficiencies in the area of men. These women did not have husbands, and we regarded them, because of this, as second-class citizens.

The degree of our integration into patriarchal heterosexuality, and conventional wisdom about the 'proper' nature of a grown-up person, is a tribute to, and reflection upon, the homogeneity of our backgrounds. Nothing, and nobody, seriously suggested to us that life was not about the formation of conventional nuclear families and the acceptance of bourgeois values and aspirations. The school's organisation further shaped our rejection of the unorthodox and the different by making the academic life so apparently alien and so much at odds with ordinary life that none of us chose it or even admired it at the time. Rather than giving us a space in which, as girls, we could develop our own interests and our own sense of self identity without masculine intrusion and masculine control, we developed, in its absence, a fascination and a respect for the masculine. The school's denial of the female body, particularly the denial of physical function and personal narcissism, gave us a sense not of the unimportance of physical appearance but of its centrality in adult relations. Indeed, many of the stated objectives and attitudes of the school to the body and personal appearance produced the immediate, and opposite, effect. As we were told to renounce vanity, so we brought mirrors and spent our lunch hours practising the art of fixing false eyelashes. As we were told that only vulgar women (and certainly not English ladies) were interested in dress, so we brought fashion magazines to school and made endless pacts with the devil to exchange our grand-mothers for the face of Bardot or the clothes sense of Jacqueline Kennedy. And as we were told that sex was nothing to be silly about so we became definitively silly about the mention of any sexual function or relationship. The mere mention of a bridegroom or a honeymoon could send the more modest spirit red in the face with embarrassment and the more frivolous into fits of giggles. In all, we disbelieved, rejected and scorned more or less everything we were told about the body and the notion of the feminine.

The school and its pupils were, of course, doomed to irrecon-cilable difference. The school, and the staff, had had to battle for existence against the conventional notion of femininity. Conven-tional women were not educated and thus we were participating, like it or not, in a tradition which was about the rejection of one aspect of convention. However, since the secondary and higher education of girls in England had been organised along the existing pattern of the education of middle-class boys, what we were being given was a model of education in which the feminine had had to be excluded for reasons of survival. We absorbed without thinking and without question the class basis of the grammar school. But we rejected the masculinist organisation of the school, while at the same time embracing with enthusiasm the notion of the masculine and entirely stereotypical ideas

71

about the power and the sheer interest of men. We had a great respect for the young, married women on the staff and entertained a romantic fascination for the teacher whose fiancé had been killed in the Second World War. This particular woman continued to wear her engagement ring (some eleven years after the death of her would-be husband) and our fantasy about her was that she continued to pine and mourn for her lost love. I eventually mentioned this view of the great unhappiness of this woman to my mother. She snorted derisively and told me – in one of those amazing revelations that make up adolescence – that this bereaved heroine was 'carrying on' with a master at the local boys' public school. 'You needn't worry about her,' was the verdict on my sad tale.

I took the advice, but at the same time I became even more baffled by the complexities of the adult world. What bothered me in particular was that this woman seemed perfectly happy, indeed she was – compared to some of the staff – positively jolly. She occasionally sported a rather dashing shade of lipstick and had once been seen, on a school trip, to order a gin and tonic at the end of what must have been a desperately tiring day. So here was someone who was perfectly comfortable in two worlds: a successful teacher and a success in a world of adult sexuality. For all that, she was not a popular teacher. Successful certainly in that she demanded and received excellent results. But far from popular in that her self-assurance and worldliness were a daily challenge to our desperate lack of both. We found her difficult in that she did not tell us how to be like her, nor did she suggest to us a means of reconciling dislike of the school and its practices with our aspirations to a wider social world. In our minds our girls' school was 'no place for a woman'. What, we asked, was a woman doing in a place like this? We were there because we had to be and because the class status of being at grammar school cancelled out many of the school's other deficiencies. The staff were there because they had no option: women graduates had little choice of career and teaching in a girls' grammar school was a better fate than many. Yet to have options and still be there defied explanation.

The explanation that we might have received and which might have opened up for us new and vital possibilities was that women could create viable and creative communities independent of men. But this argument was as singularly absent as the recognition of the female body or an assertion of the potential strength of women. No feminist point, however limited and conservative, was ever put to us to suggest that the social organisation of sexual difference had been challenged by women, and challenged in order to provide provincial adolescents with a secondary and higher education. From the school's point of view this absence is understandable, since identifying with feminism would not have fitted in well with conventional expectations. What happened, therefore, is that we assumed our teachers and their aspirations developed out of some perverse desire to be 'like men'. We were not told, and did not comprehend, that education for women had been fought for. Our imperfect logic assumed that because our teachers were failures in a sexually competitive world they remained spinsters and had to go into teaching as a poor (very poor) alternative to real life. Thus we located commitment to teaching and the academic world entirely in the failure of the appeal of the body. Like generations of chauvinists before us we assumed that education de-sexed women. Only our social ambitions – for entry to a professional world and the world of professional men – saved us from rejecting out of hand the possibilities of education and the academy.

4

Women in Uniform:
Mechanisms of Power and Control

Of the two sexes, it is widely assumed that it is men who choose to live together in institutions and communities. Men have, generally, backed up this assumption by practice and organised themselves into military institutions, schools, universities and religious houses. Long before women even went to school, men were living together in the celibate paradises of Oxford and Cambridge, and taking to those august locations the habits and experiences of an all-male public school. It is still the case that many upper-class Englishmen can pass from cradle to early adult life without ever meeting, let alone living or working with, females other than their mothers or nannies. Nevertheless, it is still supposed that while this is quite normal, indeed the conventional pattern for gentlemen, there is something rather peculiar about a lot of women living together. Where women have done this (most typically in the West in religious orders) they have been supposed to have done so under duress. No right-thinking or 'normal' woman would choose, the argument continues, to live in an all-female world, removed from men and the conventional form of female life, which is that of marriage and the home.

But if this was conventional wisdom, it was only partially correct. No doubt some women did live in convents out of constraint, but others lived there out of choice and a history remains to be written of those women, like the Beguines of mediaeval Europe, who chose to live with other women and deliberately constructed worlds which were exclusively female.

Numerous individual women chose freely to live with other women, and found in female friendship or in close relationships with their female kin associations of perfect harmony. Nevertheless, as sexual norms became increasingly rigorously heterosexual in the nineteenth century, those whose job it was to police social and personal morality became increasingly concerned that where women did live together nothing 'irregular' occurred. In her discussion of feminism and sexuality in the late nineteenth century, Sheila Jeffreys, describing the work of the historian Lillian Faderman, writes:

> Faderman explains that women's same-sex friendships came to be seen as a threat in the late nineteenth century as the women's movement developed to challenge men's dominance and new social and economic forces presented middle-class women with the possibility of choosing not to marry and be dependent on men. She sees the sexologists who classified and categorised female homosexuality, including within it all passionate friendships, as having played a major role in discouraging love between women for all those who did not want to adopt the label of homosexuality. Another American feminist historian, Nancy Sahli, shows how the outlawing of women's friendships was put into operation. In American women's colleges up until the late nineteenth century, the practice of 'smashing', in which young women could pursue their beloveds with gifts and declarations until their feelings were returned and they were 'smashed' was perfectly acceptable. These friendships were gradually outlawed and rendered suspicious by college heads who were often living with women they loved in passionate unions themselves. By the 1890s it was seen as necessary to root out these practices as unhealthy practices.[7]

The argument is thus that the expansion of education for women (particularly those forms of education – boarding schools and higher education – which led to an increase in institutional living for women) was accompanied by a self-consciousness about the kinds of friendships that might flourish in an all-female environment. Suspicions about the awful possibilities inherent in communities of individuals separated from their families were voiced by teachers, parents and many ex-pupils. For example, in Dorothy L. Sayers' detective novel, *Gaudy Night*, the heroine is finally persuaded into marriage by her experiences of life inside an all-women's Oxford College. The experiences – which revolved around foul deeds in the common rooms – were presumably not all that common in Oxford between the world wars, but what the novel does tacitly imply is that somehow or other *all these women* went slightly off their heads by living together.

The culture which produced this fear and suspicion of friendship and association between women was a culture which was fearful of any form of homosexual behaviour, be it that of men or of women. Yet if both men and women were supposed to direct all their erotic feelings and actions towards the opposite sex, homosexual activity for men, particularly upper class male adolescents, was regarded as relatively normal. The 'passionate friendships' between male members of the Bloomsbury group did not detract from their latter prominence nor attract to them the label of 'abnormal'. Nobody, for instance, expressed (at least in writing) the view that Keynes should not advise the Treasury or take a major part in British economic policy because he had had male lovers. Women, on the other hand, were likely to attract odium and social ostracism for similar behaviour: the double negative of being both female and sexually abnormal was thus a persuasive reason for women to be more circumspect in their behaviour than men. Otherwise they might well fall into the category of 'female homosexuals' so vividly described by Havelock Ellis in 1897:

When they still retain female garments, these usually show some traits of masculine simplicity, and there is nearly always a disdain for the pretty feminine artifices of the toilet. Even when this is not obvious, there are all sorts of instinctive gestures and habits which may suggest to female acquaintances the remark that such a person 'ought to have been a man.' The brusque energetic movements, the attitude of the arms, the direct speech, the inflexions of the voice, the masculine straightforwardness and sense of honour, and especially the attitude towards men, free from any suggestion either of shyness or audacity, will often suggest the underlying psychic abnormality to a keen observer.

In the habits not only is there frequently a pronounced taste for smoking cigarettes, often found in quite feminine women, but also a decided taste and toleration for cigars. There is also a dislike and sometimes incapacity for needlework and other domestic occupations, while there is some capacity for athletics.[8]

We knew nothing, in the innocent provinces of the 1950s, of Havelock Ellis and his views on women who could tolerate cigars. The name Havelock Ellis would have meant nothing, I suspect, to a single person in the school. But everyone in the school, from the Headmistress to the most junior new girl, knew about the implications of being too 'boyish' or being too fond of other girls. So influential were the views of Ellis et al. that the association of women with women for such ordinary and mundane activities as theatre-going or shopping were regarded with suspicion. The fear of lesbianism – or more precisely the fear of being labelled a lesbian – was sufficient to produce distance and deliberate coolness between friends and a wariness about friendliness shown by members of staff. Again, few of us knew, until we were well into our school career and at least fifteen or sixteen years old, of words such as 'lesbian' but we knew that there was something a bit peculiar about women being too fond of each other.

So the first rule of the school that we learnt was that affection and friendship had to be structured and expressed according to a precise set of rules. The printed rules of the school (about wearing our hats and such like) were handed to us on the first day and we were expected to observe these regulations to the letter. But also handed out to us, in a far more subtle, yet much more powerful way, was the rule about other girls and relations with the staff. Nobody said to us that an expression of affection for a fellow pupil was wrong, but we learnt that while it was quite acceptable to admire the senior girls, and mimic their ways, we were not expected to show similar enthusiasm for our peers. The labyrinthine ways of how to be normal, or how to pass as normal, were absorbed by all of us quickly and with no difficulty. The ways of 'ordinary' sexuality were contradictory and inhibited, but they were clearly marked. Rule one was that love, in any romantic or passionate sense, was about mothers, fathers, close kin of either sex and men in general. Love was not, very adamantly not, an emotion that 'ordinary' people felt for people of the same sex. When I went up to university a female friend of mine, in describing the relationship between two women, said quite casually that 'of course they loved each other'. I remember the feeling of shock that here was the expression of the forbidden. My friend thought nothing of her statement, but I remember it as a point of crossing into another, wider, assumptive world. It was not, after all, that we provincial liberals did not accept homosexuality. As sixth formers we had agreed that Oscar Wilde had had a most unfair trial, and a teacher of English had once come quite close to admitting that E.M. Forster's personal life had not quite been that of the man from the Woolwich. But these eminent men of letters were excused their sexual choices – and I strongly suspect were excused precisely because they were eminent men of letters. After all, *The Importance of Being Earnest* was a standard school play, so its author had some powerful credentials to cancel out his dubious sexual habits. We were not encouraged to read *The Importance* as an attack by Wilde on young men being manipulated out of friendship with other men into marriage by powerful women, but we were encouraged to read Wilde and regard his persecution as unjust.

Since it would have been impossible (and remains impossible) to study English literature in any detail and not come across male authors who were homosexual or bisexual we came to accept this human possibility. But we did not encounter, and were not encouraged to encounter, the alternative possibility – that of close, and possibly sexual, relationships between women. The women writers of the nineteenth century who constitute the core of the narrative tradition of the English novel (and O and A level courses) lived lives that were above reproach. Jane Austen spent her life living with her mother and her sister, the Brontës lived at home and only Charlotte married. Mrs Gaskell was the respectable wife of a minister and even the deviant George Eliot conformed as far as possible to all the conventional norms of Victorian life. All these women could be talked about without a blush on anyone's cheek. If, years later, it did emerge that Charlotte Brontë's brief marriage had brought her little happiness and that George Eliot, deeply self-conscious about the irregularity of her relationship with George Lewes, had distorted many of her natural inclinations to fit in with conventional morality, then these possibilities did not worry us at the time. These women, like Queen Victoria, had lived as ordinary women, and located their sexual and romantic passions strictly within heterosexuality. What was acknowledged, and acknowledged as fine and entirely worthy, was love between sisters. The affection between Jane and Cassandra Austen, and between the Brontë sisters, was spoken of with respect, as a perfectly legitimate and acceptable form of love. The dark side, the other possibilities, of these relationships (Cassandra Austen's jealous guarding and destruction of Jane's letters, the masochistic pact between the Brontë sisters in terms of their status in the Brontë household and in their relationship to their brother Branwell) were not part of the agreed syllabus. But nor were they part of any syllabus in Britain in the 1950s: this was a decade untouched by feminism and deconstruction. We read *Jane Eyre* in total innocence of the possibility of sexual metaphor. To us, Mr Rochester's fall from his horse was quite simply, and literally, an accident. We knew nothing about, and were certainly not encouraged to consider, the metaphorical implications of an 'accident' to a powerful male figure, nor the equally rich possibilities of the physical deforming of the same character.

In this literal world we learnt, largely from the pages of English literature, about the nature and possibilities of human love and affection. In the interpretation of the great canon that we were offered the moving emotion in adult human sexual relationships was that of love between people of the opposite sex. 'Good love', like 'good sex', was about people like Darcy and Elizabeth, or Dorothea Brooke and Will Ladislaw. This was all right and proper and suggested a neat coincidence of interests, habits and competence that appealed to our sense of order. These couples had – as the marriage manuals of then and now say – 'a great deal in common'. Having 'a great deal in common' meant that the two parties came from similar backgrounds, espoused common beliefs and shared a moral understanding. Fortunately, in fiction this perfect congruence sometimes occurred between men and women. Since we all believed in fiction, and particularly in great nineteenth-century narrative fiction, we all believed that this was the state to which we should all aspire. Being a 'good' adult meant fitting into a world in which marriages were made between men and women and involved both parties in reciprocity and support. Being a 'bad' adult meant being a greedy wife (like Rosamund Lydgate) or a silly woman (like Mrs Bennett). When George Bernard Shaw wrote 'The English who invented the horseless carriage have now perfected the sexless marriage' he was summarising the stated aim of marriage that we learnt at school. What he left out was that we were also learning about not just sexless marriages, but sexless lives. Ideally, sexual feelings did not exist, or only existed for brief, uncomfortable moments, such as in adolescence or on honeymoons. Otherwise, the world got on quite well without these uncomfortable, passionate feelings.

Yet as sex went underground, and as we learned that rule number one of the school was never to be in love with anybody but boys and men, so sex and sexuality became more powerful and deeply charged. Our community was not closed; as day pupils we all went back to our nice, normal homes every evening. Consequently, our passions and friendships did not have that all-encompassing quality which they might have done at boarding school. Nevertheless, for most of us, school was one of our two realities – we were either at school or at home, and since we spent a long day at school, and then went home with school work to do, school was a major organising force in our lives. For most of us, the friendships that we had at school were the only friendships that we had. We were not friendless, but we had few opportunities for forming alternative social networks. Every morning, just as we saw the same members of our families at breakfast, so we saw the same faces at the same desks at school. We hung up our coats on 'our' pegs in the cloakroom, in exactly the same way as we went home in the evening to 'our' bedrooms and our particular spaces in our houses. Order and regularity were the pattern of our lives, and anything that interrupted this world was regarded with general excitement. Yet beneath this absolute order and calm there existed, if not deep passions, then at least personal dramas and personal feelings. These took the form of romantic feelings for each other and concern about our ability to construct for ourselves the kind of social identity that we wanted. It was here that we learnt the second unwritten rule of the school: we must act as autonomous, independent individuals who nevertheless think only of the good of the community. Just as we were not supposed to love each other, so we were supposed to be constantly aware of each other and to act with unselfish devotion to two powerful generalised others: the good of the school and the good of ourselves. In many cases the interests of these two others coincided. For example, it was in the interests of both ourselves and the school for us to do well in our examinations. On the other hand, it was in our interests, although not necessarily those of the school, for us to apply ourselves to our task with some devotion. We were therefore encouraged to do well at examinations, but we were not encouraged to be what the English describe as 'swots'. Becoming too preoccupied with academic work was largely frowned on. It led to an unhealthy incarceration in libraries and studies (as opposed to fresh air) and a cultivation of the self that came perilously close to narcissism. We were repeatedly told that thinking about ourselves too much was a sign of selfishness and self-absorption. It followed that thinking about our work was equally suspect. Doing it – and doing it conscientiously – was one thing, but doing it with passion, involvement, commitment was quite another.

This controlled, and controlling, attitude to our work illustrates one of the features of English grammar schools that makes them, and their products, so instantly identifiable. We were there, at school, in order to learn skills and a particular range of competence. We were there, in occupational terms, to learn how to be good nurses and teachers, reliable mothers and serious-minded organisers of voluntary organisations. We were not there in order to learn about how to write (or want to write) *Othello* or *Middlemarch*. We were told to admire these artefacts of culture, but the culture within which we lived repudiated and denied the general relevance and interest of these works. We did not, therefore, study either work as elaborations on general themes about the human condition (themes such as sexual desire, sexual jealousy and the need to construct a social identity) but as particular histories of particular people. As such, as the history of a particularly jealous man or a particularly zealous young woman, the works could be understood as case histories of individuals. Indeed, the teaching we received about these works reversed what I would argue is the actual relationship in them between the general and the particular. Thus we learnt that Othello was in some sense peculiar because he was so misled by Iago about his wife's fidelity. Equally, we learnt that Dorothea was an exceptional young woman in her desire to play a creative part in the world. Jealousy, sexual love between adults, creativity and the need to be socially effective, all these motives in human existence became extraordinary.

The two unwritten prohibitions of the school – not loving each other and not thinking too much about ourselves as emotional beings – thus formed a powerful sanction against the consideration of human emotional reality and in favour of a conception of ourselves as individuals destined to carry out certain tasks. Too much introspection, too much emotional involvement (and certainly misplaced emotional involvement), and any recognition of the generality of sexual desire and human emotional complexity would have seriously threatened not only our health, but also the stability of the community in which we lived and worked. The health of that community was actually founded on the commitment of women staff to the education of women and to the establishment of educational opportunities for women. That this commitment involved a certain affection for women, if not love in the explicitly sexual sense, was not something that could be made apparent within the culture of normality and conventionality that the school endorsed and adopted as its *raison d'être*. To have loved each other would have challenged this culture, just as unbridled enthusiasm for academic work raised the spectre of the blue-stocking and a concomitant contempt for the ordinary skill of the ordinary world. Thus excellence as defined by the standards of the University of London's examining board was a convenient, institutional, measure of excellence. It was a measure that was entirely predictable (our teachers could, and did, predict our performance in public examinations with endless accuracy) and it was a measure that had all the hallmarks of total respectability and orthodoxy.

The powerful unwritten rules of the school – both of them essentially about not getting too 'involved' or too 'committed' – prepared us for adult life in middle-class England. Too much passion, either for another human being or for intellectual work, would have unbalanced the stability of ordinary life, which depended upon the individual performance of allocated tasks. Those endless sayings about 'if a job's worth doing it's worth doing well' and a 'fair day's pay for a fair day's work' were not actually engraved above the school's Honour Board but these values were enshrined in the institutional practices of the school, which put a great store on the fulfilment of allotted tasks, however mundane or however apparently pointless. A major part of our socialisation was therefore learning about the order of bourgeois life. This did not involve an education in the mechanisms of the cash nexus, but it did involve, centrally, a gradual integration into the social mechanisms and social processes that made possible the orderly functioning of capitalism and the moral and social order of the market economy.

To supply this education the school provided three sets of exercises, all of them policed in various ways. The first was the education in the thankless task. The second was the education in obedience to rules and statements by authority and the third was the independent performance of allocated work. The education in the thankless task began on the day when we arrived at school, and we learned that all of us, whatever our interests and inclinations, were going to spend a year's lessons in Domestic Science smocking a pinafore. This task was so utterly, wildly and absurdly redundant that it remains in my memory as the definitively ridiculous task. The pointlessness of the task lay, first, in the fact that after this first year very few of us were going to have any more lessons in Domestic Science, since after the first year we would begin to take additional courses in foreign languages. So here we were, attempting to learn this intricate art in order to make a garment that we would never use. We were not encouraged to view smocking as part of the great folk art

83

tradition of English life, or some such worthy, liberal, interpretation. On the contrary we were quite explicitly told that our performance at this task would be taken as a measure of our 'patience' and our ability to do something called 'work steadily'.

So for over forty weeks of my first year at grammar school I, and my ninety equally sausage-fingered contemporaries, sat in various degrees of mutiny attempting to make a couple of yards of green gingham into a garment worthy of William Morris. We nearly all failed and completed the year's work with pinafores that we were told to throw away when we arrived home – if we had not done so on the way home. The agony of the exercise was not so much that smocking was particularly boring or hard, but it was forced, and it was forced at a pace that frustrated all natural interest and inclination. One interpretation of the exercise could have been that the school was attempting to educate us in contempt for traditional female crafts. This argument was not, I think, the case, largely because the school did not see smocking or embroidery as a distinctly female art-form, as might be the case today. What was at stake in the exercise was educating us in doing something that we did not want to do. If we were too impatient in our attitude to the task, or mutinous, then it was assumed that there was quite a good chance that when faced with other, equally mundane and pointless, tasks we would simply walk away. It was an initiation, painless enough perhaps, into the hierarchy of a world that was essentially about the obedient learning of views about the world.

Our moral capacities assessed through the pinafore exercise, the first year was also the time of the moral evaluation of our physical selves. For first year girls at the school there was a peculiar on-going examination of our posture. This did not involve any specific allocation of time-tabled lessons, but it did involve the assessment throughout the year of our posture by the staff. At the end of the year the upright would be awarded with a posture stripe. This piece of blue bias binding could then be sewn on to our navy blue tunics and was supposed to indicate that we – with the blue stripes – walked like proper, upright human beings and not like the slouching chimpanzees who did not have these precious blue stripes. Again, the moral implications of the test are, in retrospect, transparent. The slouchers, the round-shouldered and the generally physically incompetent all turned out to correspond more or less exactly to the girls who had already been detected as a) having the 'wrong' attitude and/or b) coming from the wrong kind of home. The most primitive kind of physical moralism was involved here: anyone who slouched about or who sat sprawled at her desk was clearly dissolute. With the enthusiasm of the most authoritarian military regime the school watched for the signs of sloppy behaviour and sloppy thinking that might be detected in a misplaced elbow or a lounging pose. Since we were girls we could not be told to take our hands out of our pockets, but we could be told to stand up straight, sit up straight and never, ever, sit with our head in our hands. Such a posture would mean goodbye to the posture stripe forever, or the sarcastic comment that perhaps our neck could not support our head unaided.

Standing up straight, looking people in the eye and sitting in a chair as if it was an ejector seat were all the marks of a well-behaved, sensible person. No wonder that James Dean and Elvis Presley were such threats to the physical standards of the English middle class. Not only did these men slouch about, and even positively sprawl, but they could display the most unfettered masculine competence for all this bodily decadence. Unlike the (literally) upright chaps in uniform who constituted the standard, ideal pose for white English people these men walked, talked and sat with a minimal order and a great deal of impact. Inevitably, we adored them and found in their relaxed postures and physical confidence something utterly seductive. Unfortunately, such admiration was not shared by the staff who saw in these different attitudes to the body a suggestion of disorder and sensuality that was threatening. Not only did our heroes seem comfortable in themselves, they also seemed at one with the object world. I remember being told off at school, endlessly, for sitting on desks and leaning against walls. As far as I was concerned these physical objects were part of my environment, for me to use. I had no real intentions (if many fantasies) about destroying any of my physical surroundings; I just wanted to lean against the wall. Marlon Brando, Humphrey Bogart and James Stewart, I noticed, quite often leaned against walls and sat on desks.

But not in my school; we were taught respect for walls and desks. These objects were government property, not body props for idle little girls who could not stand up straight unaided. We were encouraged to view the physical world with – if not veneration, then at least respect. Again, we were children of a generation that had seen the wholesale physical destruction of whole British cities. Our school, and our homes, were close enough to London for us to know exactly what bomb sites looked like. The staff at the school had been fire-watchers through the Second World War and for them our careless attitudes to desks and other items of school property must have seemed almost irreverent in the light of their own recent experiences of loss, or potential loss. The casual view of property that we saw in Hollywood films was something that must have seemed deeply alien to our elders. In those days mass production was certainly a reality, but mass availability and mass consumption had not yet given the physical object the kind of fleeting importance that it was later to acquire in more affluent days. We expected, and were expected, to mend our clothes and take our shoes, watches, satchels and whatever else to specialist people who would mend them. We did not discard easily and thoughtlessly cheap watches or laddered tights. Perfectly respectable and comfortably-off women still mended their stockings in those very recent days.

In all, therefore, we learnt to be careful, and continent, in our physical behaviour and attitudes. Posture stripes were the way in which we would integrate ourselves into this understanding and the proper physical presentation of ourselves. It was commonplace enough – these were still the days in which models in *Vogue* stood bolt upright in photographs of couture clothes. It was not until the 1960s that Anthony Armstrong-Jones, David Bailey, Terence Donovan et al. began to take photographs that suggested physical ease and permissive sexual messages. A photograph in *Vogue* by Armstrong-Jones in the early 1960s of a model sitting sprawled on a chair wearing a bikini was hailed as a major innovation in fashion photography. To us, sharing between thirty or so of us that one copy of *Vogue*, the photograph was part of that novel, casual chic that we were trying hard to emulate. That model would never have earned a posture stripe and she, and others like her, became our guides and our objects of admiration. Questions about the arrangement by a male photographer of a woman for the male gaze did not enter, let alone bother, our innocent heads. As far as we were concerned, that girl sitting on that chair in her swimming costume was liberated in a way that we were not.

Casting off the rigid contours of the physical world was part of the process of emancipation, and possible emancipation, that we learned as we progressed through the school. From the early days of an intense desire to conform to the school's view of the 'good' body, and do well in games and gymnastics, we were gradually re-educated, by a culture different from that of the school, into a perception of our bodies as possible objects of desire. Posture stripes meant nothing to us by the time we reached the sixth form, although we well knew that down there, in the subterranean world of the junior school, were people who still believed in these marks of approval. By the age of fifteen or sixteen however, we had moved into a new phase of our careers; as the most elevated coterie in the school we were now thought capable of performing independent, and non-supervised, tasks. Yet before reaching this superior status we had passed through the intermediate stage of school life, the stage in which the written rules and regulations of the school had held sway. The rhythm of our lives in the school thus followed the pattern of wholesale, undifferentiated, integration (the posture stripe and the sewing of the pinafore) in which we were judged by absolute, unwritten, standards through to the stage of learning the details of how to behave and finally to learning how to behave independently and autonomously.

The intermediate stage of our school careers began in the second year and continued until we had taken O level examinations. These four years were the years that I remember as the years of endless tasks, endless homework and endless learning at an agreed and homogeneous rate. We learnt the school rules in this stage of our careers; indeed, at the end of our first year we were given a list of the school rules to read and absorb over the summer holidays. The end of the novitiate had prepared us for entry to the 'real' work of the school. Such was the academic organisation of the school that we spent much of our first year doing little except the most elementary reading, writing and mathematics. Since the school was taking in pupils from a variety of primary schools this exercise was perfectly sound: what was behind the very limited curriculum of the first year was the understanding that some primary schools were a great deal better than others, and that children who had attended fee-paying primary schools would have some advantages over others. When I entered grammar school in 1957 the class size at the local state primary school was on average between thirty-five and forty; the local private primary school (which I had attended) had classes of between ten and fifteen. Inevitably, the private primary school did well in terms of eleven plus results and would send to grammar school at least three-quarters of every class. Equally inevitably, the local primary school managed to send on only four or five children each year. Those children were exclusively middle-class children, whose parents (through ideology, poverty or whatever else) had chosen to educate their children at state primary schools.

So a considerable number of the first year pupils at my grammar school had attended private schools. In the first weeks at school we were able to say that we had already 'done' History, French and Latin. Since our primary schools were largely geared towards preparing boys for Common Entrance examinations to public schools at the age of thirteen we had all – girls and boys – begun lessons in Latin and French. On arrival at grammar school we discovered that these subjects would not exist for us until the following year. The esoterica and exotica of Latin, Greek, Spanish and German, along with the specialist sciences (as opposed to the 'General Science' that we all took in the first year) were only introduced to us after we had passed through the first year of socialisation and institutionalisation. This pattern of institutionalisation was, I later discovered, common to all organisations and communities. I discovered it first when I saw the film *The Nun's Story*. Although much preoccupied with the issue of the relationship between Audrey Hepburn and Peter Finch, we did not fail to notice that the career of Audrey Hepburn in her convent corresponded to our career at school. The first year was all floor-scrubbing, menial work and learning the proper deportment; only in the second year – the stage of the postulant – did the nuns start to pursue specialist tasks. So it was for us, and to this end the last weeks of the first year contained endless tests and examinations as we were divided into graded groups for particular subjects. Even though we had been assigned to different classes on our entry to the school, differentiated on the basis of our scores in the eleven plus, our primary identity in the first year had been that of 'new girls'. Within this category there were few distinctions of academic competence and ability. Only after those fateful tests in the summer term of our first year did we acquire specific academic labels: we became part of the First Division for English, or the Second Division for Mathematics. Three classes were divided into four sets for all subjects except Games, Gymnastics and Religious Knowledge. Subjects relating to the body and soul could clearly be taught to the undifferentiated mass.

With our list of school rules we therefore took home, at the end of our first year, information about which division we were going to be in. Now the world was getting serious, for being in one or other of these divisions actually had consequences for the kind of subjects that we were taught, who taught us and the examinations that we were allowed to take. Although the A stream entry was largely the core component of Division One (and the B stream the core of Division Two) there was a certain amount of cross-stream division. Some A stream pupils found themselves in Divisions Two and Three for Mathematics and a few C stream pupils found themselves in Division One. However, most of the mobility was downwards: C stream pupils seldom moved up, and they were, for the most part, confined to Division Four, with Spanish as their second language and taught by the most junior, temporary or incompetent teachers. Being in Division Four also meant that the chances of taking a significant number of O levels was limited and that any serious lapse in academic performance would put you in something called the 'Remedial' class. This group of outcasts was taught subjects called 'Remedial English' and 'Remedial Mathematics' by whoever happened to have the time or, I strongly suspect, the lack of power within the school to avoid the task.

When our parents opened the letter from the school about our academic prospects they reacted with the indifference, pride or resignation with which they generally regarded their offspring. However, in a few cases of downward mobility parents objected. Relegation to Division Two was viewed by these parents as an insult to their social honour and status. What was striking about the system, therefore, was that parents could protest about the academic judgment of the school on social grounds and have their objection sustained. A friend whose father strongly objected to his daughter being placed in Division Two because 'she would no longer be mixing with A stream girls' was not told to go away and mind his own business but actually had his objection sustained. This example of parental power is the kind of instance that must bring mixed joy to a Thatcherite heart. Here was a man invoking the crudest kind of class snobbery and having that attitude endorsed. In effect the school was saying that it too regarded it as unfortunate that people from different backgrounds had to mix with one another and that as far as possible they would recognise the importance of maintaining social distinctions.

What the school did not maintain – and if it had then it (and hundreds of other English grammar schools) might have belonged to a completely different tradition – was that its essential business was education for a meritocracy. The school could, and did, rely on the predictability of the English class system to sustain a more or less perfect fit between class and perceived intelligence; when this correspondence broke down it became apparent that class divisions within the school would be maintained. And so my friend remained, struggling, in Division One for Mathematics. But parental class-power had triumphed against the academic judgment of the school. At the same time what had triumphed was male class-power against female lack of power. However powerful our teachers were within the school they were, after all, 'only' women and therefore had none of the 'real' social power and prestige of that group known as 'our fathers'. Between 'our fathers' and the teachers there existed a curious tension. We acquired our social prestige and status (or lack of it) from our fathers and yet our fathers were part of a world against which many of our teachers had battled. If our teachers controlled our day-to-day world then it was our fathers who could, on occasions, control the school and question the autonomy of its arrangements.

Thus 'parent power' had precisely the kind of reality in the English provinces in the 1950s that sections of the Right would presumably like it to have today. It was not a democratic power, concerned with a battle for resources or equality of opportunity. Far from it, it was a class power about maintaining, not challenging or diminishing, social inequality. Our parents could, and did, rest confident that in general the school fulfilled the class expectations of the middle class. They could rest equally confident that in conflicts between academic and social judgment, it would be social judgment that would win the day. Because the class and status assumptions of the parents of the pupils at the school so closely corresponded to those of the staff there was little conflict between staff and parents on matters of social judgment. The parents could rest assured that the staff were, like themselves, middle-class people with middle-class assumptions, and the staff could rely on the parents to agree with their definitions of 'badly behaved' or 'wearing unsuitable clothes'. What school and parents did not have to deal with were those vexed issues about different cultures, different manners and different understandings of the social world that have come to beset English state education.

So when we arrived home with our list of rules, or our circular letters from the Headmistress, the reception was generally one of (fairly) serious attention. The list of school rules began with the general ('Girls must behave in a way that maintains the good name of the school') but very rapidly, that is by Rule 3, lapsed into the particular. The particular rules involved never going upstairs on buses (since they were apparently dens of iniquity, or more precisely men smoking cigarettes), always wearing our school hats in the streets, never walking along a pavement more than two abreast, never, ever, eating in the street, never going outside in our indoor shoes and never bringing into the school either sweets or books or magazines that were not part of our school work. We were also not allowed to wear coloured underwear of any kind, shoes with heels or any jewellery at all. This last rule attracted some heart-searching on the part of the school, since what it effectively banned (along with the rings, bracelets and necklaces that we longed for) were the crosses and

91

chains that the more pious among us had a taste for. Despite the fervent protestations of piety and spiritual sincerity that went with the defence of wearing these items the school stuck to its guns: jewellery was jewellery and a rule was a rule. Watching children come out of secondary school in the 1990s, wearing fashionable clothes and jewellery, and rushing upstairs on buses, it is astounding to think that a mere thirty years ago, on the same planet, children (and their parents) had sufficient respect for and belief in a rigorous dress code to observe the rules and regulations of full uniform.

So the list of rules included about ten items that were specifically about uniform and dress. What was surprising about this list, apart from its existence, was what was left out. We were not told that we could not wear make-up or pierce our ears; it never occurred to anyone that we would do these things. Such behaviour belonged to a grown-up, adult world of which we were not part, and which we had no hope of belonging to until after we left school. Our childhood, as far as the school was concerned, was to be endlessly extended until we were adults. Being a teenager as magazines and comics were beginning to describe adolescence had no interest as far as the school was concerned. The experimentation of adolescence, the mistakes with clothes, make-up and social behaviour, all these things were not to happen and they would not happen, we were indirectly told, if we followed the school rules and did not do any of the slightly deviant things that the school rules brought to our attention. As far as other possibilities were concerned – real social deviance, rejection of the school and its code of manners and major deviations in dress and behaviour from the generally agreed norm – these outrageous acts did not exist. The contract between us, the pupils, and the school was that we would maintain the surface, apparent normality and in return would be allowed the kind of autonomy that is given to the well-behaved patient or prisoner.

Our institutional career thus followed the classic institutional pattern of novice, learner and senior, trusted inmate. Being in the sixth form was the point of crossing the line. No longer one of 'them' we became part of the adult, serious school. Our individual personalities suddenly became a matter of interest and our tastes and inclinations became matters of conversation and even of mutual exchange. We became university and scholarship 'material' – no longer troops to be trained, we became the human potential that might vindicate the system. It became apparent that as far as the school was concerned the previous five years of our lives had simply been basic training. Once we had taken O levels we had, in effect, earned – or not – our commissions. If we passed our seven or eight subjects, and still managed to turn up at school every day wearing more or less the right school clothes, then we became, quite suddenly, officer material and entered the glorious freedom of the sixth form 'rooms'. To return to school after O levels and enter the sixth form was to enter a different world. From being relegated to a downstairs classroom in which our desks were arranged in formal rows we were able to walk up the central school staircase to rooms where we could choose desks, desks that were arranged informally and were essentially places in which we would do 'our work'. It dawned on us that in this new world we were not going to be taught in the same way; rather than being presented with a beginning of term timetable that looked like a model for the short-sharp-shock of reform school we were presented with something called an 'outline of work'. The school day, and the school week, apparently had gaps in it. Time took on a different dimension. No longer was every minute between 9 a.m. and 4 p.m. accounted for and arranged for us without our consultation; now the days contained great open vistas of space called 'private study'. There remained the compulsory games and religious education, but the rest of the time was devoted to the study of subjects of our choice. Our choice of subject was related to the sympathy and liking we felt for individual teachers. We could at last escape from the sarcasm or rigour of the staff we disliked. No more miserable hours wrestling with the isosceles triangle, no more dreary hot afternoons drawing oxbow lakes and writing down the ninety-six features of market gardening in the Thames Valley. Now all was to be the chosen subject and the chosen person.

It was entry to the sixth form that convinced me that adults were correct in saying that life gets better as you get older. I had not dreamt that life could get this much better and the years in the sixth passed, if not in a frantic whirl of happiness, then at least in reasonable contentment with part of my immediate surroundings. At last our Pilgrim's Progress was rewarded with entry to heaven and a release from the mundane trials and tribulations of earning and proving our place in the world. We had made it: we had demonstrated that we could survive initiation and could learn rules. Our reward was that now we were largely allowed to police ourselves and take part in the policing of others. It was thought unlikely that girls in the sixth form would actually want to commit the acts of minor deviance that so beset the junior school. We were regarded as old enough to change our shoes, to wear our hats and to adopt what was regarded as the 'sensible' attitude to the rules – that of resigned toleration. In exchange for this resigned toleration we entered into a compact with the staff and we were allowed to know the inner secret of the rules: that they were there for maintaining the order and the cohesion of the community rather than for any good, practical reason. Allowed into this freemasonry, we were then expected to adopt an 'adult' attitude to the rules. Being 'adult' and being 'sensible' were now the words that were used to praise our behaviour. Maturity was the new goal.

Since we were regarded as mature, or potentially mature, adults we were given the responsibility for helping to maintain order. As trustees we were, in effect, allowed some of the keys to the outside world; we were certainly allowed to demonstrate to the girls of the junior school that authority and maturity were possible goals that they might grow towards. In order to demonstrate that we were now trusted pillars of the community the school made about two-thirds of the sixth form into prefects. This policy had the effect of distributing power so widely that it hardly mattered; equally it had the effect of defining as totally, irretrievably and utterly beyond the pale the girls who were not made prefects. I remember that of all the moments of terror in my life none was worse than waiting to hear whether or not I had been made a prefect. Since it was not a rare prize, it became much more important to have this dubious honour. If only a few of us had been blessed with authority, then the rest of us could have laughed off the whole exercise. As it was, we were paralysed with fright that our past misdeeds would suddenly catch up with us. Would they remember the false teeth produced in the music class; would they somehow just know that we had frequently come to school wearing black underwear? All these dreadful acts of deviance assumed a new importance as the list of the saved was read out. Audible sighs of relief could be heard as we knew that our heaven, which we had waited so long for, was going to admit us as chosen beings. As prefects, we could enter the pearly gates of the sixth form as the redeemed and the blessed.

On the other hand, if we were not prefects we entered the sixth form almost by default. Becoming a prefect gave us two distinguishing marks of dress: we were expected to sew blue braid all round our blazers and we were allowed not to wear hats in summer, although we were still expected to wear the loathsome velour *chapeaux* in winter. The chosen were thus immediately distinguishable. We could now back-comb our hair as high as the sky without any fear of our labour being squashed under a hat and trailing blue braid sagged around the sleeves and lapels of our school blazers. Probably we looked more of a mess than the rest of the school. Needless to say, this hardly mattered. Whatever we looked like we were allowed to report the misbehaviour of other pupils, we had a room of our own and we were assumed to be free from the possibility of sin. The non-prefects in the sixth form, the submerged third, lived in a moral twilight compared to our radiance. Their misdeeds and their misbehaviour had clearly been remembered, and must have been so gross as to disqualify them for ever from the ranks of the elect. It did eventually dawn on some of us that the non-prefects were more often than not the girls who were described as 'not university material' and that being made a prefect had more to do with the school's perception of what would be acceptable to university admissions officers rather than of any totally objective assessment of virtue. It also became transparently clear, within days of arriving in our sixth form heaven, that being 'university material' was what it was all about. Either we would make the honour roll at the end of the school hall, or we would leave to do something useful, but not worth the school's expenditure of gold paint. In those long gone days making the honour board meant gaining either (or both) something called a county major scholarship or a state scholarship. State scholarships were abolished in the year that I entered the sixth form and many of us swots felt much like the ambitious person suddenly hearing that a socialist government has abolished hereditary peerages. Posterity would now never know, we argued, that we could have gained a state scholarship. Our names would pass for ever into oblivion or the comparative mediocrity of county major scholarships.

However, even if we were not going to make the gold paint at the end of the school hall, we were going to go to university and we were the trusted guardians of the order of the lower school. To us fell the supervision of the queues at lunch, we were expected to parade the cloakrooms at lunch time, to make sure that no junior person malingered in the locker room rather than enjoying the fresh air. It was our duty to ensure orderly behaviour at bus stops, on buses. Our policing function did not end when we left the school, but extended to the world between the school and the home. I doubt if we were expected to exercise authority over junior pupils not in uniform (and thus not likely to bring disgrace on the school) but we were expected to make sure that anyone in the school uniform behaved themselves in the proper way. If we chose to report someone then we were to do so via the prefects' book – an exercise book kept with the Keeper of the Sixth Form, an august Senior Mistress. What was remarkable about this book was that it remained forever empty. None of us ever reported anyone. This was due less to a fear of a possible lynching if we did grass on any of our near contemporaries than the generally impeccable behaviour of the school as a whole. Nobody did anything worth reporting. Whether from fear, lack of imagination, total, numb passivity or whatever else, the school behaved with endless obedience to the expectations of authority. The most deviant act committed during my seven years at school was not perpetrated by a member of the school, but by an evil outsider. This evil outsider (in the shape of some boys from the local boys' school) poured red ink into the school swimming pool the day before the school sports. We were encouraged to regard this desecration as an act of vandalism roughly equivalent to the bombing of Coventry. Even a twitch of the face that might indicate amusement was immediately forgotten at the sight of the awful wrath on the face of the Headmistress. We were cowed by her evident fury and watched in amazement as the boys' Headmaster (a senior and respected teacher who was at the time Chairman of the Headmasters' Conference Schools) came to apologise formally to our school. The extent of the possible delinquency of naughty boys was forever engraved on 600 impressionable minds. What happened to the criminals themselves I do not know, but if discovered they presumably underwent an experience that must have combined being cashiered, black-balled and excommunicated.

By comparison with this misdeed, not changing our shoes was hardly worth mentioning in the same breath. Middle-class girls have never been known for their deviance; we were no exception. Our worst failings (in the eyes of our teachers) were failing to work hard enough and having too little school spirit. It was on this latter score that we were most generally and seriously deficient. Few of us had any school spirit and however passionate our friendships we were, in the masculine sense, 'unclubbable'. Although divided as soon as we entered the school into four houses (named after four famous men!) there was almost no one who had any enthusiasm for the fortunes of 'her' house. I can remember, I shall never forget, the name of my school, but I cannot recall whether I belonged to Morris, Constable, Byrd or Spenser house. In theory we had competitions between houses at games and scholastic achievement; in practice we had almost no sense of this competition. If being a prefect was to be deeply desired, then being a House Captain was to be avoided at all costs. It was an office that was regarded as fit only for children or idiots; anyone who could believe in the glory of the house had real problems about their relationship to reality. We distrusted absolutely the school's attempt to create what we regarded as false unity. Although we could respect the unity of the school, the artificiality of the house system was an anathema to us all.

Nevertheless, the office of House Captain was a category and a rank that existed and one that four unfortunates had to undertake. Two other offices completed the list of our sixth form hierarchy, those of Head Girl and Deputy Head Girl. Over these appointments we had no control, but the tradition of the school was that the Head Girl should not be an academic 'high-flyer'

What was being confirmed in this office was not the academic, but the moral order of the school, and to this end the school separated, and brought to our attention the separation of, virtue and wit. 'Be good sweet maid and let who will be clever,' was a motto that our teachers were fond of quoting. Indeed, the Headmistress wrote this saying inside my last school prize. (Thus I have a copy of *Ulysses* with a warning against the sin of knowledge inside the front cover.) So the Head Girl was not the Cleverest Girl but the Best Girl, and as such stood a good chance of winning the school's most important prize – the Service to the School Prize. This prize was awarded each year to the most morally competent of the pupils. The qualification for winning the prize was conspicuous service of a caring kind. The school maintained, as our later experience might have contradicted, that care for others and selfless altruism would be rewarded. It was generally the case that the Head Girl won the prize, but this was not inevitably the case. In my last year at school the prize was won by a particularly stolid citizen, a girl with little standing among her peers. Such awards presumably served to maintain hope among the pupils that virtue would be both noticed and rewarded. Again, there was a motto for this kind of service: 'They also serve who only stand and wait.' As a prescription for the kind of passive femininity that brings with it few rewards and the likelihood of endless exploitation it was a motto which we generally mocked. Our petit-bourgeois experiences and backgrounds might warn us against the dangers of intellectualism, there was no such resonance on the subject of suffering and quiet accommodation to the world. Our world, our future was to be made; that, we realised from our first day at school, was what selective education was about.

5

Life Scripts

Those of us who left school in 1964 were almost the last generation of state-educated children to be educated in the rigidly tripartite selective system introduced by the Butler Education Act of 1944. Although the eleven plus still exists in a tiny number of English counties the country as a whole had 'gone comprehensive' by the end of the decade. Selectivity and division were maintained, but maintained by means other than a brief examination at the age of ten. We had been educated in a self-confident system, and were made to feel constantly aware of the privileges that we had enjoyed. We were also made to feel that access to selective education, and particularly higher education, was a matter that rightly entailed scarcity. The post-Robbins assumption that education was a right to be shared as fully and as widely as possible was largely absent from the environment where we spent our adolescence. We were encouraged to view our grammar school as a scarce resource, which might be deserved but which did not necessarily have to be shared or extended to others. As *'la crème de la crème'*, as Miss Brodie was fond of describing her sixth form pupils, our sights were set (or expected to be set) on entering even more exclusive institutions of educational privilege than the one we already attended.

Going to university was thus the expected goal of all sixth form pupils, the *raison d'être* of the two years of intense study of three subjects. In those days this ambition had not yet acquired a general currency among the English middle class, and the figures on university entrance corroborated the common-sense impression that going to university remained relatively rare. In 1963/64, when we were poring over university prospectuses, the new universities had yet to be established, or were little more than building sites, and policies on equal opportunities had not even been conceptualised, let alone implemented. As girls, even middle-class girls, our chances of getting into university (particularly to read subjects such as medicine or law) were not as good as they were to become ten or twenty years later. Even if our chances were better than the mythical working-class girl in the Robbins Report who had a 1 in 600 chance of going on to higher education, entry was still highly selective and very competitive. Despite the fact that we were used to this (indeed we had just spent seven years being educated into the idea that education necessarily entailed selection and competition) it was nevertheless a daunting prospect to be told that two years' hard work and blood, sweat and tears over A levels could come to nothing. If we failed to make those coveted A level grades of at least three 'C's then we would be forced back to the ranks of training college applicants. There were few polytechnics to offer us alternative places, and we came to realise that conditional offers from universites meant precisely that.

The endless hurdles of middle-class life had been introduced to most of us in childhood. We had all been brought up knowing exactly what we were allowed to do at a particular age, how we had to work hard at school to pass the eleven plus and how we then had to work even harder in order to stay at grammar school and pass our O levels. Then, surprise, no surprise, as soon as we had taken those exams new ones arrived on the scene. If we passed those exams, and passed them well enough, we were then given the licence to go and take more exams. The future stretched before as an endless succession of hurdles. Some of these hurdles were, we realised, public examinations. The other hurdles were the life events that we dimly, and not so dimly, realised were part of the process of becoming fully fledged members of the middle-class community. Among these hurdles were getting married, buying a house, starting a family and making sure that the children went to good schools. This, we knew, was what the future was all about, and learning to be competent at all these decisions and processes was an important part of our education. If our competence, or our judgment, failed then we could easily find ourselves married to the wrong person or living in the wrong house with too many children, all of them at inadequate schools. In those days nobody had ever dreamt of CSE or GCE examinations in the 'Quality of Life' or 'Health Education' or any of the other subjects which today teach and try to instil 'proper' values in adolescent heads. But even if this formal education in the values of the middle class did not exist, the informal education was there, and centrally so.

In learning about what to be when we grew up we were expected to come to appreciate order, emotional continence and self-discipline. The organisation of the school put a daily stress on the orderly and systematic presentation of self: the neat appearance, the performance of standard, daily tasks and the continuity of effort. Working hard was generally expected, but more than that we were expected to work hard consistently. The stress was less on the furious energy of creative activity than on disciplined, consistent application. The kind of inspired and obsessional energy that is sometimes associated with an individual's commitment to a particular task was less favoured than diligent, steady work. The fable of the hare and the tortoise was much favoured as an illustration of the virtues of plodding away. A criticism frequently levelled at those of us more inclined to the hare's approach to life and work was that 'She can certainly work when she wants to.' The implication of this remark was that for most of the time we might be bone idle and shiftless, but faced with a task in which we were interested we could complete it with speed and dedication. Unfortunately, such an approach did not fit in with the school's rhythm of work, especially in those years before O level when teaching and learning were more organised and controlled than they were to become in the sixth form. One of the greatest tortures of those years before the sixth form was reading texts in English or French literature classes. This exercise was equivalent to the agony of being shut in a room with a dripping tap. The process went thus: every academic year had different texts assigned for reading. Usually, we read two novels, one Shakespeare play and a number of poems each year. The agony lay in taking a year to read the text, and knowing, as the leaves fell in September that we would have to live through autumn, winter, spring and most of summer before we reached the end of *Mansfield Park* or *Henry IV Part I*.

As a means of alienating generations of schoolchildren from the classic literature of Europe this method was one of unmatched success and brilliance. By the time the days lengthened and we changed out of blue serge winter uniform into our blue gingham summer dresses we no longer cared what happened to Fanny Price or Falstaff. We just wanted them to go away. The utter absurdity of the method reached its pinnacle in the year that we took O level. Our set text for the English novel was (what else?) *Jane Eyre*. But by the time of the examination we had not, at least officially and in class, reached the end of the novel. Those immortal lines of 'Reader, I married him,' were still far away from our eyes. It was only through the devious, but not altogether uncommon, method of finishing the novel ourselves that we went into the examination knowing that Jane Eyre and Rochester were eventually united in one of the great world historical defeats of the male sex. Many of my contemporaries must still be wondering what happened at the end of those popular classics of the nineteenth century. I remember in particular that *Vanity Fair* – a very long novel – was left unfinished about half way through. It was not until some years later that I read the second half of the novel and discovered the nature of the resolution of the plot.

But this form of reading, while it alienated and bored, had the great virtue from the point of view of the teacher of allowing her to know exactly where everybody was in terms of information and progress. The measurement was exact: everybody was on page 41, or whatever else it happened to be. That was one virtue of the system. The other virtue of the method was that in a curious, and subtle, way it drew attention from the work as a whole, and translated it into a task, a set of exercises that the novelist completed. We gained little understanding of the text, since in many cases we never read all of it, but what we were being taught was a lesson in detailed construction. The vision, and the understanding, of the novelist was less important than her ability to provide coherent sentences, realistic descriptions, pithy remarks and all the other apparent indications of a great novelist. Our attention was drawn in every lesson, in every tedious encounter with the daily three-page allowance of Austen or one of the Brontës, to the skills of the novelist, and in that sense we were certainly being educated and taught something about English literature. But what we were not being taught was how novels (or poems or plays) are conceived, constructed *and* completed. The centrality of the ending in any understanding of a text was absent from our lessons; this centrality, I suggest, might have posed awkward questions about the nature of the artist's intentions. To fragment a work of fiction or drama into a number of constituent parts is to encourage the appreciation of skills at the cost of the appreciation of vision and purpose. We thus left *Jane Eyre* having no idea about Charlotte Brontë's devastating critique of Victorian ideologies of femininity and duty. In the same way we left unfinished Thackeray's ironical conclusion to *Vanity Fair* and his less than entirely enthusiastic comments about Amelia Sedley. Our attention was drawn away from these problematic ideas, and directed instead to the more obvious skills of the novelists at writing dialogue and illuminating human character and motivation.

The way in which we were taught literature, and particularly English literature, was not in any sense eccentric or exceptional. Judging by our excellent results in public examinations we were being taught exactly what examiners wanted to read. Even if we had little idea about what happened to Jane Eyre, Falstaff et al. we could write with fluency and precision about characterisation and the use of metaphor. Moreover, we had been taught to recognise the moral implications of the English novel, and we reiterated our received impressions in our examinations. It was an approach to English literature which treated fiction as a more sophisticated version of the children's fable. Educated as children through the fables of Aesop and the equally moralistic tales of Grimm and Hans Christian Andersen, it was a short step to an understanding of literature which stressed the same endless defeat of the bad by the good. It was certainly true that we understood that the good had to struggle, indeed suffer, to succeed in the end, but eventually all was well. Moreover, all ended happily because the 'good' characters maintained their integrity and always acted well. It was a version of fiction in which choice and constraint were virtually abolished, as were the intentions of many novelists to show the ambiguity of human moral choice and the complexities of motive and action. The novel, like life, was thus a Pilgrim's Progress in which the 'good' person plodded on from beginning to end.

The correspondence of this version of fiction with the expectations of middle-class life was one which made English Literature a highly significant subject within the curriculum. Teaching us Science, Mathematics, Geography or History depended to a great extent on teaching us facts: we were in those classes to absorb information or learn methods and skills. In English Literature however, we were learning about life; more specifically we were learning about how to live. What we were being taught was the not altogether unreasonable lesson that if we did the 'right' (or conventional) thing, then we would be all right in the end. The essential moral that we were taught was that right, and good, were the normal, conventional actions and attitudes. Thus if we were always unselfish, polite, hard-working, honest and deferential then we would be rewarded. This lesson was very far from misleading: polite, hard-working and honest middle-class children *could* expect to reap a rich harvest of rewards. There was little in our experience to suggest that the world was a place of endless negotiation, in which rewards were unreliable and not always distributed with absolute attention to moral worth. Even though we were the children of parents who had lived through a world war (as such we were the famous 'bulge' generation) and even though our parents had been part of a generation that had come close to devastation, the fundamental self-confidence of our middle-class homes and backgrounds had not been shaken. Indeed, such was the strength of the British mythology about the triumph of the Churchillian spirit over the evils of Fascism that the self-confidence of the middle-class world in which we grew up was much enhanced. Hitler had been defeated; but so too had Attlee, and the 1950s had seen the return of those class distinctions in appearance and experience that had been a temporary casualty of the war years. In these years of peace it was perfectly legitimate to expect that we would be able to inherit, if not the earth, then at least our share of our parents' mortgaged home and white-collar expectations.

The revolution in the curriculum in English schools from the late 1970s was to introduce schoolchildren to characters whose experience of life was, if not broader, then at least different from that of the provincial middle class. We remained, however, firmly rooted in a tradition which located all fictional human experience in the progress towards a middle-class home. Dickens, Austen, Charlotte Brontë were all about the establishment of the 'good' home, the home in which the central values of bourgeois existence were to be lived out and reproduced. It was our responsibility to learn those values, because we, as wives and mothers, would be responsible for instilling them in the next generation. Equally, if we did not learn to be unselfish, thrifty and hard-working then we would not become the ideal home-makers of the bourgeois world – the wives who believed in home cooking, regular meals and unselfish devotion to the interests of husband and children. God forbid that we should grow up to be interested in such frivolous pursuits as clothes, dining out or the risks and uncertainties of creative intellectual life. 'Duty' as portrayed by Shakespeare in *Henry IV (Parts I and II)* and *Henry V* was the standard which was set for us. The speech in *Henry IV Part I* in which Prince Hal explains to the audience (school parties everywhere) his attitude to Falstaff and his youthful indulgences ('I know you all, and will awhile imitate the sun') was a speech which was much favoured for discussion and examination. Literature as text – in the sense of a text for a sermon – was a dominant teaching mode.

The mode of proceeding through the great works of English drama and European realism was one which stressed the orderly reading of the work. We began at the beginning and we dutifully read on. Our part in this ritualised consumption of literature was to learn from the texts presented to us each week and to produce well-written explanations and demonstrations of our under-standing. What we were supposed to understand was that the necessary characteristics for a fully successful integration into the adult, bourgeois world were those virtues of order, emotional continence and self-discipline. These characteristics were all demonstrated in those characters in fiction and drama who were regarded as excellent sterling characters. Men and women like Mr Knightley, Fanny Price and David Copperfield all plodded on, putting aside the temptations of personal inclination, short temper and self-indulgence. Even faced with situations in which they stood to lose a great deal, they behaved with a stiff upper-lip courage that embodied all that was best about behaviour. Expressing your emotions, particularly through public grief or anger, was a taboo that had to be learned. At best, our teachers were allowed to be 'annoyed'. Thus if some rule or expectation had been flouted the language of admonition was phrased in terms such as 'I'm really a bit annoyed with you', or 'I'm rather cross about this.' Never were we to receive the suggestion that the staff were furious, or close to murdering any of us, or indeed anyone else.

The suppression of anger in women has become a phenomenon identified by recent feminist therapy as one of the (many) causes of depression and low self-esteem in women. To be unable to express anger is thus no longer seen as a strength but as a weakness, since without (to use the jargon) 'coming to terms with anger' individuals turn upon themselves the irritation and the anger initiated by the behaviour of others. Yet suppressing anger was precisely what we were taught to do. To have a 'temper' was regarded as a major character flaw, and one that had to be unlearned. But the confusion that existed in this teaching was less about what was 'good' and 'bad' in terms of emotional health than about the equation of anger with dissent and rebellion. Anger was interpreted as a fundamentally disruptive form of behaviour. Angry people, it was quite rightly assumed, shouted, expressed exaggerated opinions and generally disturbed the spirit of compromise and ambiguity that was regarded as the proper form of social life. If people did get cross, then it was assumed that there must be some explanation that was unrelated to the theme of their anger. That is, people might get angry if hot, cross and tired but they should not get angry about matters of principle or feeling. One of the much loved texts of the early years at grammar school was *What Katy Did*. What Katy did was repeatedly get cross, and learning to control her temper was part of her voyage to maturity. Indeed, North American nineteenth-century heroines must generally have been a quick-tempered breed, for exactly the same moral lesson was the fate of Jo in *Little Women*. English heroines were, to judge by the pages of fiction, a less impetuous and unruly collection.

So unlearning the feeling of anger was part of our education. No doubt this lesson was not generally successful, for the generation of girls who left school in the early 1960s managed to get rather successfully angry on occasions about such diverse targets as the war in Vietnam and various aspects of sexual inequality. Yet these distant targets (even if they did have immediate personal implications in some cases) were perhaps less problematic than the assertion in interpersonal relationships of personal interests and rights. The equation that we were taught (that being angry was the same as being violent) did not stand us in good stead for asserting our rights against individuals as diverse as husbands, university tutors and shop-keepers. 'The English never complain' is a cliché about national characteristics that has been corroborated by the evidence about the unwillingness of the English to condemn poor service and inadequate goods. These aspects of life – largely concerned as they are with consumption – are important; more important as far as individual women are concerned is the learned unwillingness to complain about marital violence, sexual harassment and manifest discrimination. We were not told that any such things existed; this might not have mattered if we had been encouraged to learn a form of self-assertion that was about more than the individual demonstration of our talents. The expectation was clearly that through showing the world that we were 'good', tidy and excellent at examinations, the world would respect us and our talents. Unfortunately the world often showed a marked incapacity to appreciate any of these excellent qualities. Which left us with few resources. Given the continuity and the predictability of the English class system few of us landed anywhere except on our feet. Nevertheless, that happy landing was often through neither wit nor design, and for those who did not get washed up onto the comfortable shores of the next generation of the middle class the fate was likely to resemble that of the heroine of Fay Weldon's novel *Heart of the Country*. This heroine – a woman with two young children – is suddenly abandoned by her husband and finds herself with no money, no job and no pair of shoes serviceable enough for walking. Our school taught us the value of sensible shoes, but this lesson was entirely literal, there was no teaching in the metaphorical importance of sensible shoes for life.

The social contract which this teaching assumed was one in which desirable virtues were recognised and rewarded. It was taken for granted that anyone who behaved, and acted in correct ways, would reap, if not immediately then at least eventually, a rich harvest of social respect and material success. The good, the elect, of the English middle class could expect both to go to heaven and to achieve heaven on earth. In the late 1950s this expectation was entirely reasonable; the post-war consumer boom and the immediate post-war years of limited unemployment and increasing private affluence had provided the middle class in general with a comfortable and secure way of life. These were the years before the war in Vietnam, before the sexual revolution and the 'permissive society', long before the overthrow and disappearance of many traditional codes of class behaviour and patterns of deference. Perfectly respectable middle-class people spoke unashamedly (as did the Harrods catalogue) of 'nigger' brown and the working class did not share, and were not expected to share, tastes such as foreign travel or the consumption of wine. This class lived in council houses and were only to be met in hospital waiting rooms and bus stations. One of the apparent traits of this class was that its members tended to shout (as at football matches and in industrial disputes) and the prohibition on anger and raising the voice certainly had quite a lot to do with the fear of suddenly being seen to revert to a primitive social state. The class fear of becoming declassed was thus fed and fuelled by the gendered fear of being unlady-like. The two dominant fears were inseparable: it was just as bad to be declassed as to be thought unlady-like. Both states were equally bad, and the learned discipline of keeping one's temper was essential to maintaining that gendered class identity.

However, even if we were not allowed to be angry, emotion still had to be expressed. Since we could not legitimately rant, rage and fume we turned to sulks, silences and sobs. The sulk became an endlessly used mode of resistance; even if it did not take the form of total withdrawal and refusal to participate, it did take the equally subversive form of refusal to cooperate in the values of the school and the popular mythology of the willing participant. The most common examples of the subversive sulk were the deliberately failed academic test and the deliberately dreadful participation in games or gymnastics. One adolescent Schweik of my recollection could reduce to total and absolute fury the senior gymnastics teacher. This good woman expected complete enthusiasm for jumping over stuffed horses and climbing ropes. Unfortunately, it was not a general skill or a general enthusiasm. Nevertheless, the teacher expected a fully committed performance from all of us and with quiet sarcasm would berate less than perfect renderings of these skills. This criticism sometimes hurt, more often infuriated. Since we could not answer back, we deliberately did badly. But some chose to do badly with a taste for the dramatic. These girls would take a furious run at the stuffed gymnastics horse and then, as if by magic, suddenly stop and with an expression of acute existential doubt on their faces, scratch their heads or adjust their clothes. The teacher would rant and rave, but short of carrying the offending pupil over the horse herself, she had no way of achieving the perfect results that she wanted. What we had learned by this point was subversion, and mild, childish and silly as it was, it was an exercise with heady possibilities. We knew that we could not be punished for scratching our legs or blowing our noses and we also knew that we could provoke the other person into stepping into the position of being in the wrong. Every time the teacher lost her temper, we won. Like the central character in *The Loneliness of the Long Distance Runner*, who finally refuses to cooperate with the aspirations of the staff of the borstal, we knew that the staff depended upon us for their status as teachers of model grammar school pupils.

This game of getting our own way, and controlling situations where we did not share the values or behaviour at issue, was used as endlessly in the classroom as it was in the gymnasium or on the games field. The classroom offered less immediate scope, since the tests set to us there were more widely endorsed and more difficult to make appear ridiculous. Even so, the deliberately misread poem, the flat rendering of the Shakespearian speech and the total lack of interest in the results of experiments in Physics and Chemistry were all part of a challenge to the expectations and aspirations that we were expected to share. The tight-rope that we learned to walk was one between absolute failure and absolute success; we knew, and we knew that they knew that we knew, that if we could be good enough, and good enough when it mattered (that is, in public perform-ances and public examinations) then we could sulk, fail to perform and behave inadequately at other times. It was an expectation that suggested a model of human behaviour that was profoundly poorly integrated, in that the accepted mode of behaviour was one of achievement in relationship to an external stimulus and not from a particular motive or developed interest. The school and the staff expected us to perform properly when confronted with stimuli as diverse as the gymnastics horse or GCE examiners; this method of organising our behaviour had the very great virtue, from the point of view of school and society, that the stimuli could be controlled, changed and reorganised as the values and interests of society changed. Our parents had lived through an excellent version of this blue-print for social life in the Second World War: defeating the Germans had become the national aim and all behaviour was expected to be organised in relation to this end. We no longer had to defeat the Germans, but we did have to do well in examinations and learn how to demonstrate our skills when presented with particular tasks. What we did not learn to do was to find out much about our real interests or talents; such a process would have been infinitely disruptive and anarchic, quite different from the orderly social world that we were being educated to take part in.

It would, of course, be romantic to suppose that among this generation of schoolgirls (or indeed any other) there lurked dozens of great artists, writers, scientists or musicians. It is not, therefore, that genius was suppressed and thwarted. But what did happen, repeatedly, was that confusions were made about what particular individuals could, and would want, to do. For example, girls who were labelled as 'quiet' were thought of as good future librarians, presumably on the grounds that people are not expected to talk in libraries. Any girl who was more than competent at academic life was marked out as a future teacher, in the same way as neat and tidy girls were typed (as it were) as secretaries. The exceptionally determined stuck to their guns and went their perverse ways to modelling academy and the London School of Economics, but these choices were regarded as errors of both taste and judgment. What was curious about the school's view of our futures was that it was founded on a fundamental lie: we were told that we had to get worthwhile jobs, yet no one expected us to stay in paid work for longer than a couple of years. A pointless sense of order was, I think, largely what was at work in the scripts that the school wrote for us. It did not matter that in the case of girls the nature of the academic order was largely irrelevant and superfluous; again (as in the case of learning how to be a properly behaved person) what was important was class-based social order. The central requirement of the school was that we did well, or at least performed properly, when we were asked. On the whole, given the nature of our social backgrounds, there was a close correspondence between the school's expectations and our behaviour. Our departure from the values of the school was only ever minimal and our rebellion limited. Certainly, we never answered back, or openly defied our teachers, or refused to do as we were told. Tales of pupils at other schools who smoked in the cloakrooms, talked in class and generally misbehaved were tales of another, exotic, world as far as we were concerned. A friend of mine had a mother who taught in a local secondary modern school and when this woman told us, with some wry amusement, that a favourite pastime of the more delinquent pupils in her class was to unscrew their desks, thus causing the general collapse of the classroom furniture, our imaginations were seized by yet another of the world's amazing possibilities.

Reliable schoolgirls that we were, the staff of the school could relax in the certain knowledge that only quite exceptional provocations would cause us to become seriously troublesome. There were two ways in which trouble was going to be caused, and these two causes were well known. The first was the presence in the school, or an individual classroom, of a 'trouble-maker'. This kind of person incited dissatisfaction and generally set a bad example. Trouble-makers could normally be identified by their attitude to boys (excessive enthusiasm), academic work (lack of interest and untidy presentation) and the importance of the good name of the school (derision). A constant threat that we were presented with was that of the pollution or desecration of the good name of the school by some thoughtless or evil-minded individual. The argument went thus: if you wear your beret in that generally sloppy fashion then it will be assumed that we all wear our berets in a sloppy fashion and the entire school will become known as a community of badly dressed sluts. The movement from the one badly placed beret to the damnation of 600 other people was fast, but apparently unstoppable and automatic. We all belonged to that community, and the good name of the institution was our individual responsibility. These 'good name' arguments are much beloved of the European bourgeoisie; military organisations, professions, residential communities all rely upon, and put a considerable importance on the fulfilment of certain standard external requirements. The individual and the whole stood in the kind of relationship that is the dream of Fascist governments; our relationship with the school was unmediated by an infrastructure of sub-groups, minorities or alternative cultures and as individuals we all carried the responsibility for the corporate group. Any failure to conform to corporate expectations thus made punishment immediately possible, and beyond *rational* explanation or justification. The way a beret is, or is not, worn is a matter of supreme insignificance in any real educational sense. Rationally, therefore, there was nothing to punish. But irrationally, in terms of that bourgeois compulsion towards the ordering and conformity of the complexities of psychic and social reality, the matter of correct dress and correct behaviour had a major importance.

In making the demands of us that it did, the grammar school acted out that function of the father ideal which Freud identified as central in social organisation. Writing in *Group Psychology and the Analysis of the Ego*, Freud argued that:

> All individuals' private emotional impulses and intellectual acts are too weak to come to anything by themselves and are entirely dependent for this on being reinforced by being repeated in a similar way in other members of the group.[9]

We would certainly have been able to do nothing in the world without the seven years of secondary education that we received at grammar school. At the same time what we did after we left school was shaped by those seven years. We did not enter the school entirely unformed; by the age of eleven we had all acquired the experiences of family life and eleven years of settled, peaceful existence. But we had little understanding or knowledge of the world or, more important, any real notion of how to acquire and assess knowledge. Our 'getting of wisdom' was a process which was, in some senses, enlightening (we could hardly help but leave the school knowing more than when we entered it) but in other ways repressive, in that the organisation of the school emphasised values and skills that were to prove serviceable, but in many instances non-transferable to the world outside the school. The school's identification of the trouble-maker was in part an unstated recognition that certain trouble-makers brought into the closed community of the school issues and problems that the school would rather forget. Trouble-makers could, for example, exhibit a capacity to get by, and even do well, without following the formal rules of how to achieve correctly. The talents of the trouble-maker were deeply suspect, in that they defied the very processes of learning that the school advocated.

This individual refusal to toe the institutional line was one of the ways in which disorder was created. Equally, disorder was created by too great an adherence to the rules of the school. The alternative fascination and repulsion with order in western society was ever present in that provincial school. Expected as we were to conform we were also expected to remain individual and to demonstrate the virtues of independence and autonomy. Anyone arriving from Mars would no doubt have been staggered by this small-scale social system which demanded on the one hand obedience and on the other critical dissent. Girls who were in some sense 'too good' were regarded as creeps and teachers' pets, and condemned (by staff and pupils alike) as somehow deficient in the proper understanding of authority. The function of authority was apparently, and ideally, to make decisions *without consultation*, and to be obeyed when it gave an order. Yet we were not supposed to concur with the values of author-ity; in a curious way it was suggested that those in authority over us were also only carrying out orders and that if an alliance in terms of values was suggested between us and them then this somehow subverted the social order. Any pupil who made an attempt to cross the lines of staff and pupils, on the grounds of common cause, was therefore sharply put back in her place. What was going on here was an exercise in the maintenance of petit-bourgeois privacy (how dare we try to find out what the staff thought?) and at the same time an equally important demonstration that individuals perform certain tasks, and have certain powers, but what is to be obeyed is the institution and the function and not the person. If we tried to get to the human reality of this or that teacher then we were effectively breaking that unwritten (and written) social law which says that people have authority because of their social positions and not because of their individual characteristics.

When we entered our school at the beginning of each of our approved days we did not pass slogans or statements of our purposes. The script that we had to learn was unwritten. Nevertheless, other people have not been so remiss as our teachers. In an account of the virtues thought necessary for a work-force in industrial capitalism, E.P. Thompson, quoting the sociologist Wilbert Moore, describes the kind of behaviour that this ideal work-force is supposed to have. He writes:

> Wilbert Moore has even drawn up a shopping list of the 'pervasive values and normative orientations of high relevance to the goal of social development' – 'these changes in attitude and belief are "necessary" if rapid economic and social development is to be achieved'.

> Impersonality: judgement of merit and performance, not social background or irrelevant qualities.
> Specificity of relations in terms of both context and limits of interaction.
> Rationality and problem-solving.
> Punctuality.
> Recognition of individually limited but systematically linked interdependence.
> Discipline, deference to legitimate authority.
> Respect for property rights.

114

These, with 'achievement and mobility aspirations', are not, Professor Moore reassures us,

> 'suggested as a comprehensive list of the merits of modern man ... The "whole man" will also love his family, worship his God, and express his aesthetic capacities. But he will keep each of these other orientations in their place.'[10]

Thompson makes no bones about his dislike of Moore's values, and the values of the world which Moore endorses. But his criticism is not just of the values, it is of the social institutions that these values create and maintain. At the conclusion of the essay Thompson takes the case of education to illustrate all that is, in his view, wrong with the application of the needs of industrial capitalism to the organisation of social life. He writes:

It was Werner Sombart who – using that favourite image of the clock-maker – replaced the God of mechanical material-ism by the Entrepreneur: 'If modern economic rationalism is like the mechanism of the clock, someone must be there to wind it up.' The universities of the West are today thronged with academic clocksmiths, anxious to patent new keys. But few have, as yet, advanced as far as Thomas Wedgwood, the son of Josiah, who designed a plan for taking the time and work-discipline of Etruria into the very workshops of the child's formative consciousness ... Wedgwood's plan was to design a new, rigorous, rational, closeted system of education: Wordsworth was proposed as one possible superintendent. His response was to write *The Prelude* – an essay on the growth of a poet's consciousness which was, at the same time, a polemic against –

The Guides, the Wardens of our faculties,
And Stewards of our labour, watchful men
And skilful in the usury of time,
Sages, who in their prescience would control
All accidents, and to the very road
Which they have fashion'd would confine us down,
Like engines ... ![11]

115

But when we read Wordsworth we did not read these subversive works. As 'modern men' we were being educated in precisely the kind of skills that Wilbert Moore defined as essential for the useful member of a contemporary industrial society. Even if, as girls and women, we were going to play a domestic rather than a public role in 'modern' society the expectation was still that we would know, and subscribe to, the dominant values of the society. After all, we were going to be primarily responsible for the socialisation of the next generation, and that task should ideally be carried out by individuals already cognisant of the central orthodoxies of the market economy. Our brief, if heady moments of resistance to the expectations of the school were motivated in part by boredom and conventional adolescent dissatisfaction with the adult world, but there was an element in the refusal which was derived from an inarticulate sense of the pointlessness of many of the demands made on us and the irrelevance of many of the standards set by the school.

Judgments on our behaviour on a day-to-day basis were many and plenty. Of particular and daily importance was our ability to do as we were told and to accept that the tasks set for us were meaningful and useful. Many of the tasks no doubt were useful in that through them we acquired specific information or specific skills. But some tasks had little or no relevance to any skill or information, their importance was that they trained us to perform given tasks. It took years for me, and I suspect others, to unlearn the ever-present school expectation that a 'good' girl loved doing tasks rather than the task itself. The stress on meeting externally approved and designed targets was there before us every morning. The process left little time or energy for passionate or committed involvement in work or individual projects and it was a system which made it all too easy to do nothing if external constraints were removed. Given that most universities and middle-class careers are full of psychic – and material – whips designed to ensure performance and achievement it was inevitable that once on one of these conveyor belts we should all perform. But it was equally inevitable that what we did in those contexts should be dictated by constraint rather than by choice. The strain on individuals which this system establishes is ever-present, as is the evidence which demonstrates both the strength and the weakness of this organisation of the human ability to work and produce. People do become, in popular parlance, 'married to their careers' and other aspects of social existence, notably relationships with others, assume a secondary importance.

So when we looked at our teachers what we saw was a model of adult existence that was both frightening and unattractive. We said of our teachers that they 'only had their jobs' and we turned to the ideas of home and family as areas of richness and fulfilment. Being adult, married women seemed extremely attractive when set against the lives of the unmarried teachers that we knew. These women seemed to be concerned about little except endlessly demanding of us the orderly presentation of tasks. The quasi-rational world that they appeared to defend and represent was deficient, to us, in human interest, in vitality and in enjoyment. Where, we might have asked, is the sheer pleasure in the academic world? What is there to enjoy in these exercises and tests that we are so constantly set? We did not ask where the enjoyment lay in the rigour and draining demands of domestic life; to us that world seemed attractive compared to the endless discipline of academic work. We thus set up a mental division between the creative world and the world of the intellect.

This division was enhanced and institutionalised by the practices of the school itself. Our individual talents were, as suggested above, assessed virtually every day. Certainly, at the end of every term there were tests and more or less formal examinations. Additionally, the end of every term saw the composition by the staff of our reports. Reports were sent home to parents and contained an assessment of our performance. The judgments in these reports were partly objective (in that they gave details of the marks for work that we had gained throughout the term) but they were also subjective, in that the staff, particularly our form mistress, wrote a kind of brief character sketch about our general performance and attitude. The remarks were all written in a fairly developed kind of code. For example, 'Jane has tried hard' meant that Jane would never do well at that subject but had at least not torn up the textbook. 'Jane could try harder' meant that Jane had been seen to demonstrate considerable lack of interest in the subject. 'Jane shows promise' meant that Jane

117

was getting close to becoming competent at the subject. Nobody was ever bone idle, appalling or outstanding. The evaluation was curiously polite, often evasive and largely moral. The comment that reflected the highest opinion of the school was 'Jane has worked hard and played a full part in the life of the school.' Which was tantamount to saying that Jane has done everything that she has been asked to do and has cooperated fully in the school's view of itself. The worst comment to go home with was 'Jane could work harder.' We were fascinated by these reports, but in the fascination there lay that endless sense of possible failure. We longed for good reports, we wanted to be told that we were intelligent or promising but in the classic emotional tradition of the British love and approval were always withheld.

Trying hard at academic work did not, therefore, bring with it immediate emtional rewards. Our friends regarded us as 'swots' and the staff did not always praise us. Much more rewarding was to be good at art, or drama or dance. Excellence in these activities was all much valued by our peers; we regarded people who could paint well or play a musical instrument with recognisable competence as in some sense in touch with a creative world that was far removed from the dry discipline of academic study. In recognition of this sub-culture the school channelled off these talents into a different value system from that of the central academic tradition. The thinking was represented by the common-place remark that 'Jane is only fairly good at academic work but her painting is excellent.' Adjectives such as excellent, talented and promising – which were never used in the context of the evaluation of academic work – were scattered across the pages of reports. But brilliant talents in these areas were not recorded on the school's Honour Board and it was frequently stated that 'Art' did not count as a 'proper' subject. Indeed, for the purposes of university entrance this was perfectly true. Nevertheless, we were supposed to take the contents of the National Gallery seriously and being able to distinguish between Rembrandt and Reubens was regarded as one of the marks of a civilised person. These artists would all have had 'excellent' on their school reports, but at the same time it would have been a judgment about a secondary activity, an activity where praise was possible because the activity itself was fundamentally unimportant. Art, music, the visual and creative arts in general were part of a peripheral world. From the point of view of serious, grown-up people, only slightly mad, eccentric people engaged in life-time commitments to art, music or literature.

In Margaret Drabble's *Jerusalem the Golden* a girl from an unnamed northern city, educated at a grammar school, goes to London University and there eventually meets a family with extensive, and established, associations with the arts. At a first visit to the family's home the central character initially reacts with amazement at the rich variety of both material objects and social relationships contained within the household. Particularly striking is an ancient gilt eagle in the sitting room. It is there for no good reason, but of it the visitor remarks, 'the aristocratic ideal was vindicated.' From one point of view the eagle does nothing except collect dust and occupy space, but from others the eagle, an object of beauty and a craftsman's skill, represents a certain kind of possibility about the extent of human creativity. Needless to say, there were few eagles adorning the bare walls of my grammar school. A reproduction of Van Gogh's *Sunflowers* hung in the main entrance hall, but otherwise the corridors were bare of all visual display. In those years before every middle-class household with children displayed artwork in the kitchen there was no expectation that juvenile or adolescent work was worthy of display. 'Art' was displayed in the art room and kept there. The connections between the visual and, for example, the literary arts were thus completely severed, in terms of both their physical presence in the school and the school's assessment of their relative importance in terms of the great hierarchy of knowledge. It was probably entirely accidental, but it is impossible not to recall that the school's library was next door to the Headmistress's study while the art room was situated at the back of the school, next to the kitchen and the tradesmen's entrance. Generations of schoolgirls must still associate art lessons with the smell of lunch cooking and the clatter of vans and dustbin lids.

Given the segregation of the arts into the nether regions of the school it was possible, and common, for many of us to assume that the arts were somehow representative of all that was creative and innovative in social life. Thus the curious paradox of the school's distrust of these subjects was that a false romanticism was bred about the skills of painting or acting or drawing. Because creativity was located in these activities it was assumed that academic and intellectual life was not also a potentially creative world. The script that was written for us and for our adult lives by this distinction was debilitating in that it entirely underestimated the amount of hard, disciplined work involved in creating even the most mediocre painting and entirely over-estimated the amount of work necessary to produce a passable essay in O level History or Geography. Because disciplined work was a positive, highly rated moral quality it was constantly associated with subjects and activities where its existence was apparent. Being good at Art or Music was, by contrast with being good at History or Mathematics, a matter of natural talent or inspiration. Indeed, any creative activity was assumed to be about innate skill rather than endless hard work and practice. Thus when our creative efforts in the adult world were rejected or dismissed we assumed that we had no talent. Equally, since we had not been taught to recognise (let alone respect) intuitive rather than systematic intelligence we developed an exaggerated respect for intelligence that appeared to be endorsed by authority and social power. We left school and went to university or training college believing in, rather than understanding, the value of intellectual life. At many of these institutions standards and expectations were so closely approximate to the standards of the conscientious performance of given tasks that we had known at school that we did well enough to make the judgments of our school look respectable. Our references from universities, like those school reports, stressed that we were hard-working and diligent. We emerged into the adult world with extensive and authoritative evidence of our ability to carry out given tasks and to live a disciplined and sober life. Little wonder that many people still dream fondly of the institutions that apparently created us.

Notes

1 Brian Jackson and Dennis Marsden, *Education and the Working Class*, Penguin Books, Harmondsworth, 1966, p. 242.

2 Bernard Crick, *George Orwell: A Life*, Penguin Books, Harmondsworth, 1982, p. 136.

3 Virginia Woolf, *A Room of One's Own*, Penguin Books, Harmondsworth, 1963, p. 87.

4 Mirra Komarovsky, 'Cultural Contradictions and Sex Roles', *American Journal of Sociology*, Vol. 52, November 1946.

5 See the discussion in Elizabeth Wilson's *Only Halfway to Paradise*, Tavistock Publications Ltd, London, pp. 81–111.

6 Sylvia Plath, *Letters Home*, Harper & Row, New York, 1975, p.198; Faber and Faber Ltd, 1976, p.198.

7 Sheila Jeffreys, *The Spinster and her Enemies, Feminism and Sexuality 1880–1930*, Pandora, London, 1985, p.105.

8 Havelock Ellis, *Sexual Inversion, Studies in the Psychology of Sex*, Volume 2, F.A. Davis, Philadelphia, 1927, p.250.

9 Sigmund Freud, 'Group Psychology and the Analysis of the Ego', in *Standard Edition of the Complete Psychological Works of Sigmund Freud*, Hogarth Press, London, 1974, Vol.18, p.61.

10 E.P. Thompson, 'Time, Work-Discipline and Industrial Capitalism', in M.W. Flinn and T.C. Smout (eds), *Essays in Social History*, Oxford University Press, Oxford, 1974, p.69.

11 E.P. Thompson, 'Time, Work-Discipline and Industrial Capitalism', p.69.

Dale Spender
Invisible Women
The Schooling Scandal

With a new introduction by Sue Adler

When first published, this classic study examined the way in which women are educated, and concluded that equal opportunity was a myth.

Now, two decades after the Equal Opportunities legislation, are girls getting the same chance to excel as boys? Who gets time on the computers? If anything, women's hard-won rights to be educated seem to be under new threat, and Dale Spender's research, done mainly in the 1970s, has become more relevant then ever.

Dale Spender's many books include *For the Record: The Making and Meaning of Feminist Knowledge* (The Women's Press, 1985); *Learning to Lose: Sexism and Education*, with Elizabeth Sarah (The Women's Press, 1980) and *Feminist Theorists: Three Centuries of Women's Intellectual Traditions* (The Women's Press, 1983).

Education/Women's Studies £4.95
ISBN: 0 7043 4146 8

Pearlie McNeill
One of the Family
An Australian Autobiography

'I was an orphan, all right. An orphan with parents.'

Pearlie McNeill grew up 'a sombre, plain, introverted child'
in Sydney in the 1940s and 1950s. Her memories do not
have the cosiness of *Neighbours*, but recall violence,
deprivation, abuse and a great deal of pain. In *One of the
Family* she paints a compelling picture of her life: of loathing
for her violent father, and a blend of anger, compassion and
occasional admiration for her mother, who had very little
time for comfort and encouragement for her children
usually, but who took a neighbour to court for throwing
water over her youngest child when he peed in the gutter!

Autobiography   £7.95
ISBN: 0 7043 4210 3

Carol Jones and Pat Mahony, eds
Learning Our Lines
Sexuality and Social Control in Education

A resistance book for education in the 1990s.

Learning Our Lines documents historical and current state control over education and sexuality, and examines the disturbing link between sexual violence and social control of girls and women.

Fighting fire with fire, this study shows – in response to government legislation on education, including the Education Reform Act and Section 28 of the Local Government Act – that schooling promotes heterosexuality in which stereotyped ideas about masculinity and femininity go unchallenged and that this – and *not* the 'promotion' of homosexuality – is the problem. By looking at past initiatives and the responses of young women and teachers today, the authors offer inspiration and strategies for young people, teachers, governors and parents alike.

Education/Women's Studies   £7.95
ISBN: 0 7043 4199 9

Dale Spender and Elizabeth Sarah, eds
Learning to Lose

Sexism and Education

Revised Edition with a new introduction by Pat Mahony

Learning to Lose was a crucial book in the development of
feminist theory and practice of education.

This stinging analysis shows how curriculum material,
classroom interaction and mixed-sex schools still
disadvantage girls, while new articles deal with the
problems faced by black girls and young lesbians in Britain
today. This revised edition also includes an updated
bibliography, making it an invaluable source book for
teachers, educationalists and parents.

Education   £5.95
ISBN: 0 7043 3863 7

Maureen Lawrence
A Telling and a Keeping
A Writer's Autobiography

A Telling and a Keeping is an unforgettable portrait of the artist as a young woman, growing up in the north of England in the 1940s and 1950s.

Moving to the inescapable rhythm of home, school, home, school, and dreaming of escape through romance or university, this young woman learns that in the face of opposition silence and subterfuge may win where confrontation fails. One day, she promises herself, she will use her other voice, the voice that speaks her mind.

Maureen Lawrence is the author of two novels, *The Tunnel* and *Shadow on the Wall*, and of several plays.

Autobiography/Literature   £4.95
ISBN: 0 7043 4148 4